ORGANIZE
FOR A
MISSION

A Guide for Parents
and
Missionaries

ಬಂಡ

Marie Calder Ricks

Second edition.

Cover design and photographs
by Marie Calder Ricks.
Cover photos courtesy Mr. Mac, Orem, Utah.
Graphic illustrations ©2011
by Thomas E. Ricks,
www.tomricks.com.

Visit *www.houseoforder.com* for more information regarding your organizational needs or to purchase organizational products, schedule personal consultations, speaking engagements, or educational seminars.

Organize for a Mission,
A Guide for Parents and Missionaries
Copyright © 2011 by Marie Calder Ricks.

Printed and bound in the United States of America. All rights reserved. No part of this book may be reproduced in any form or by any electronic or mechanical means including information storage and retrieval systems without permission in writing from publisher, except by a reviewer, who may quote brief passages in a review.

Published by Marie Calder Ricks,
6756 West 10050 North,
Highland, Utah 84003.

ISBN-13 978-0-9788579-3-6
ISBN-10 0-9788579-3-3

*This book is dedicated
to the missionaries in my life:*

*My paternal grandfather,
my father, my husband, our sons,
and to each and
every other adventuresome missionary who leaves home, family,
and friends for one of the greatest
and most difficult experiences
of his or her life!*

Contributors

James N. Ricks, West Spanish American Mission

Thomas E. Ricks, Brazil Rio de Janeiro Mission

David N. Ricks, Paraguay Asuncion North Mission

Brian C. Ricks, Italy Rome Mission

Tyler M. Ricks, Brazil Ribierão Preto Mission

Candice C. Andrus, Venezuela Maracaibo Mission

Heidi H. McClellan, France Paris Mission

Eric S. Sumsion, South Korea Seoul Mission

Laura B. Tolsma, Germany Munich/Austria Mission

David L. Haden, Manager, Mr. Mac, Orem, Utah

Vaughn & Kay Anderson, former Mission President and wife of Paraguay Asuncion North Mission, and former District Presidency of the Provo, Utah Missionary Training Center

Table of Contents

"Let all these things be done in order..." D&C 58:55

Introduction iii

When the Mission Call Comes, Go to Work 1
- Dad To Do 3
- Mom To Do 5
- Missionary To Do 21
- Siblings, Extended Family, & Friends To Do 31

Items to Buy and Take 36
- Bigger Investments 39
- Clothing for Elders and Sisters 52
- Clothing Specifically for Elders 65
- Clothing Specifically for Sisters 84
- Additional Useful Items 104

Other Financial Needs to Consider 120

Preparation of Essential Kits 128
- First Aid Kit 129
- Office Kit 132
- Cooking Kit 135
- Recipe Box 136
- Repair Kit 137
- Sewing Kit 138
- Shoeshine Kit 140
- Spares Kit 141

- Vital Documents Kit 142
- Comfort Kit 143

What You Need From Home 149

Packing for Easier Travel 155

Starting Out Right, Right Away 163
- Personal Habits 164
- Exercise Habits 165
- Grooming Habits 165
- Obedience Habits 167
- Reading Habits 167
- Social Skills 168
- Budgeting Skills 169
- Shopping Skills 169
- Cooking Skills 170
- Housecleaning Skills 171
- Laundry Skills 187
- Ironing Skills 188
- Mending Skills 189

What It Will Be Like 194
- For The Missionary 194
- For The Parents 201

It Doesn't End When The Mission Does 214

Making It Easier the Next Time Around 219
- Doing Once, Twice or Even Three Times Over ... 221
- Financial Preparations For the Next Missionary 223

Conclusion 225
About Marie Calder Ricks 227
Also by Marie Calder Ricks 229

Introduction

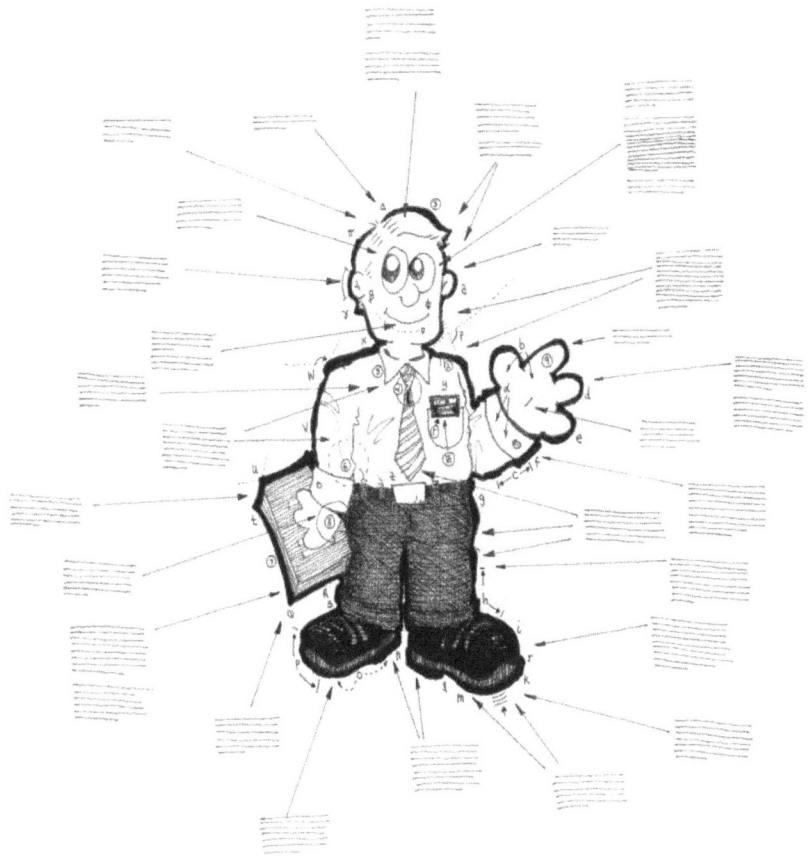

"Life up your heart and rejoice, for the hour of your mission is come; and your tongue shall be loosed, and you shall declare glad tidings of great joy unto this generation." D&C 31:3

When you are staring at the store's shirt rack wondering at the difference between broadcloth and oxford cloth... When you shop for dress slacks and consider the question, "Cuffs or no cuffs?"... When you begin packing the luggage and wonder how it will all fit in.... When you try to make sense of this exciting and yet very stressful time, it will help to have some additional insight from a professional organizer and a four-time missionary mom.

This book is an organization guide for new missionaries, both Elders and Sisters, and their parents. It will help you get organized and stay that way through this exciting and sometimes confusing time. It is a guide for making mission preparations easier, smoother, and otherwise orderly.

I wish to share my best knowledge about preparing for a mission, in addition to contributing other missionaries' experiences, and adding some advice from professionals. I have also included specific techniques for making good decisions and important, but often neglected, pointers for the alert organizer. My husband and I have sent four sons on missions. I have worked with several young women to better understand the parts of missionary preparation exclusive to them. I have listened to and considered other parent's advice and then written.

You will gain a lot of wisdom as you go through this "prepare for a mission" experience, but I am here to help, this time and every time another missionary receives his or her call. Therefore, this book is a companion to any and all information received in the Missionary Packet or from the mission president and as such, any instructions received from these sources should always supercede the contents of this book. I have attempted to be as complete and informative as possible, but understandably remove myself from personal liability for any decisions you or your family members may make during your missionary preparations.

Introduction

Organize For A Mission uses "checkboxes" for your ease in crossing off items you have considered, purchased, or gathered. Appropriate chapters end with easy-to-use checklists to further facilitate preparations for an organized missionary experience. I have also added in *italicized font* additional suggestions that might be useful. And lastly, forms and checklists in this book can be printed for personal use at *houseoforder.com/category/downloads/*.

May your mission preparations make better sense and be less expensive as you approach them in an organized manner! And may the Lord bless all our missionaries!

> *"It is wisdom... that he settle up all his business as soon as he possibly can... that he may perform a mission unto me... to testify of my name and bear glad tidings unto all the world."*
> D&C 114:1

When the Mission Call Comes, Go to Work

"And if it so be that you should labor all your days in crying repentance unto this people, and bring, save it be one soul unto me, how great shall be your joy with him in the kingdom of my Father!" D&C 18:15

Oh, the excitement at the arrival of the important news! The wonder as the letter is read and Missionary Packet reviewed! The perplexity that comes as maps are examined. The comprehension as the mission becomes very, very real! The enormity of this anticipated experience is right in front of you now. There will be much to do, much to organize, and much to arrange!

Of course, as you begin preparing for a mission, fasting and prayer are essential so mission preparations happen with the help and blessings of the Lord. Seek for guidance, ask for help in prayer, fast for direction and inspiration. This can be done again and again as you face difficult questions, consider complex situations, and make important decisions during mission preparations. Always, always look to the Lord first for help!

And then it is time for action. As preparations begin, as decisions are reached, and as essentials are purchased, it helps to be organized. In fact, some simple preparations will make this mission experience and any future missions for your family members much easier, less stressful, and more organized than you might believe. Read this guide carefully, act with wisdom, and prepare well for one of the more exhilarating experiences in life: A mission.

Each member of the family and even friends can help in significant ways once the mission call is received. Therefore, different sections of this book are directed to those specific individuals. No matter your role in the upcoming mission preparations, all will be smoother with some organization. There is much to be learned and much to put in order. Here are some ideas.

There is a section each for dads, mom, the missionary, and siblings/extended family/friends!

Dad (and sometimes Mom) –

"And the Lord said... Let them go up [to preach the word] for many shall believe on their words, and they shall have eternal life; and I will deliver thy sons..." Mosiah 28:7

❏ Missionary Packet.
After the initial excitement and shock has settled in, it is of the highest priority to thoroughly read the Missionary Packet that came with the mission call. It contains important information that will give direction to the pre-mission activities plus guidelines for specific arrangements, clothing requirements, and sequencing of priorities.

❏ Finances.
Start putting more funds aside for pre-mission expenses. It takes a lot of money to get a son or daughter on a mission and the costs of clothes, shoes, shots, and sundries adds up quickly.

You will also want to decide where the 18 to 24 monthly missionary payment funds will be coming from, calculate when the payments will begin and when they will end. Planning in this manner will help make the inevitable "sacrifice" easier on the whole family.

And while it may seen initially premature, you may want to open saving accounts for future family members' mission preparations, a topic which is discussed in greater detail in the section entitled

"Financial Preparations For the Next Missionary," page 223.

❑ Health Insurance.

Carefully read the instructions received in the Missionary Packet regarding health insurance coverage. Contact your insurance company and the Missionary Department, if required, to make the necessary arrangements and specific changes to adequately insure your son or daughter while they are absent from your home. Make sure you understand the implications of your arrangements, the Church's policy, and act wisely for the benefit of all!

❑ Wall Map.

Find and purchase a large wall map of the locality where your son or daughter will be serving, have it laminated, and post it in your home. This will make each and every missionary experience more meaningful to you and your family. These maps are usually available at local bookstores. Look online if you want maps of an area in a foreign country. Even if it is notated in another language, it will give you a good idea of distance and geography.

"All things unto me are spiritual, and not at any time have I given unto you a law which was temporal... for my commandments are spiritual."
D&C 29:34-35

Mom (and occasionally Dad) –

> *"And my mother was comforted...And she spake, saying...I know of a surety that the Lord hath protected my sons... and given them power whereby they could accomplish the thing which the Lord hath commanded them...and they did rejoice exceedingly... and they gave thanks unto the God of Israel."* 1 Nephi 5:7-9

❑ Worry List.

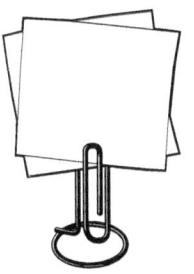

Start working and worrying, but mostly working, as the worrying doesn't help much. Set aside one place to begin writing down your worries, since you will want to find the best solutions and/or resolutions to them during this preparation time. A great place for this worry list is in the "Mission Preparations" Binder as discussed on page 10.

❑ Missionary Packet.

It is of the highest priority to thoroughly review the Missionary Packet. Because it contains essential guidelines that will give focus to your pre-mission activities, it must be digested again and again. Often for missionaries going overseas, there are additional instructions for visa and passport preparations to begin right away. It is important to impress upon your missionary the urgency of these tasks; and, that you, too, immediately begin to do as requested in the Missionary Packet, especially regarding immunizations. There are fewer challenges getting into the mission field when packet instructions are followed completely and thoroughly now!

I was always surprised, when reviewing the Missionary Packet a week or two after its receipt, at all the items that had escaped my attention the first time through the paperwork. During your second review of the packet, I suggest making a written list of outstanding, yet to be done items, so you will feel confident as you continue to prepare for your son or daughter's mission.

❏ Calendar Calculation.

Find a convenient calendar and count how many days until your missionary will depart. This will help you set some mental pacing and will often send you into momentary panic. But don't worry, with a little additional organization, all will be well as this important information will soon be formalized! See "Mission Preparations" Wall Calendar on page 16 for additional instructions.

❏ Stash Shelf.

Set aside a specific location to stash items you think should go in the missionary's luggage. Then, as you find, purchase, or think of items that need packing, you will have one "home" where you can collect and put away items until these ideas can be discussed with the missionary.

❏ Shot Records.

Find the shot records for your missionary. If you haven't been good at record keeping, this may take some doing. It is essential for the missionary's immunization records to be updated and complete so all appropriate shots and preventive medications can be given so he or she will be sufficiently protected.

❏ Thank You Supplies.

Purchase thank you cards, envelopes, and stamps. As much as possible, your missionary should have the opportunity to express gratitude for pre-mission gifts soon after they arrive and well before he or she departs. The more "thanking" the missionary does, the less will be left undone. After your missionary leaves, it will likely be you or your spouse's privilege to finish this project!

❏ Mission Announcement Letter.

Family and friends will want to know of your missionary's call. Of course, you will phone some people immediately. Others can be notified by email or letter. However it is done, this can be a time-sensitive issue, as you won't want to leave anyone out.

After consulting with your bishop (or branch president) and confirming a date for your missionary's sacrament meeting talk, you might consider an email or letter with a map and helpful information as you share the good news with all interested parties. Two example formats follow (one for an Elder and the second for a Sister).

Dear Family and Friends:

We wanted to let you know that ____ has recently received a mission call from the Church of Jesus Christ of Latter-day Saints. He will be spending the next two years serving in the ____ mission.

He will travel from ____ on ____ to enter the ____ Missionary Training Center. It is there he will learn the ____ language and prepare for his missionary labors.

He will be leaving the Missionary Training Center on ____ to begin his labors in the field and will be serving until approximately ____.

If you are interested in contacting him during his time in the Missionary Training Center you can write to:

_____
_____
_____

As only parents and siblings are allowed to communicate with missionaries by email, if you are interested in contacting him in the mission field, the address to use is:

_____
_____

Our missionary will be speaking at ____ during our church services in the building located at ____ on Sunday, _____. Please feel free to write us with any questions.

Sincerely,

Dear Family and Friends:

We wanted to let you know that ____ has recently received a mission call from the Church of Jesus Christ of Latter-day Saints. She will be spending the next eighteen months serving in the ____ mission.

She will travel from ____ on ____ to enter the ____ Missionary Training Center. It is there she will learn the ____ language and prepare for her missionary labors.

She will be leaving the Missionary Training Center on ____ to begin her labors in the field and will be serving until approximately ____.

If you're interested in contacting her during her time in the Missionary Training Center, write to:

————————
————————

As only parents and siblings are allowed to communicate with missionaries by email, if you are interested in contacting her in the mission field, the address to use is:

————————
————————

Our missionary will be speaking at ____ during our church services in the building located at ____ on Sunday, _____. Please feel free to write us with questions.

Sincerely,

The forms on pages 8 and 9 can be also downloaded for your personal use by going to http://houseoforder.com/category/downloads/.

❑ **"Mission Preparations" Binder.**

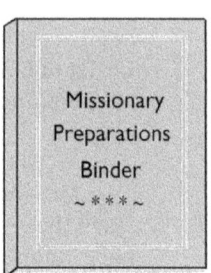

To be initially organized for your son or daughter's mission, you will need to set up several tools to accommodate planning, record keeping, and staying organized. The first tool is the "Mission Preparations" Binder, the second tools are the "Stay-At-Home" Missionary Journals, the third is the "Missionary Affairs" Binder, and the fourth is the "Missionary Affairs" Wall Calendar.

You will need:

- One 2" view binder, labeled front, back and down the spine "Mission Preparations."

- Five or more binder tab dividers. Consider buying "extended" tabs so you can see the tabs past the sheet protectors that might be used in the binder. These dividers can be labeled:

    ❑ To Do
    ❑ To Buy
    ❑ To Prepare
    ❑ To Pack
    ❑ Information

- Binder pencil holder (for collecting receipts).

- Pens and/or pencils.

- Lined paper (for making lists and written notes).

- Sheet protectors and cardstock (for keeping odd-sized items).

- 8-1/2" x 11" monthly calendars from the current month to the departure month that are three-hole punched and placed in the front of the binder (for noting deadlines, appointments, and commitments).

- 8-1/2" x 11" yearly calendars from the year of the missionary's departure to the year their anticipated return.

These yearly calendars are used for making notes about your responsibilities during the missionary's absence. For instance, you may have to activate a deferred scholarship or make arrangements for housing. You may have to renew a CD at the local bank when it matures or register for university classes. If you have a convenient calendar upon which to make your notes, it will be less likely you'll forget to act at the appropriate date and time.

I found it best to prepare a "Mission Preparations" Binder, with dividers, extra lined paper, and a pencil holder (into which I put every receipt as it seemed one or two things had to be returned during the missionary preparation process and I wanted to know exactly where those receipts were located), and several sheets of cardstock inside sheet protectors (into which I put various odd-sized documents I didn't want to three-hole punch).

Having one place to keep all the paperwork saved a tremendous amount of time while going through the "mission preparation" season. It also provided an excellent reference resource in anticipation of doing this again and again as subsequent family members or friends went on missions.

❑ **"Sentimental Activities" List.**
Begin a written list of important "sentimental" activities you desire to do before your missionary leaves. This list could be kept behind the "To Do" tab in your "Mission Preparations" Binder.

For instance, your family may want to have one last treat at the local ice cream parlor, a pizza picnic at the neighborhood park, or a casual family picture taken at the zoo. While you may not be able to do everything you desire, when the opportunity comes up to do something, you will have a written list from which to plan.

❑ **"Stay-At-Home" Missionary Journals.**
In addition to a "Mission Preparations" Binder, you will need to prepare two "Stay-At-Home" Missionary Journals. Having two journals will provide adequate

room for all the missionary mementos. These binders can immediately store those important papers that are part of receiving the call and will serve as a secure place to continue putting important missionary papers, letters, and treasures. If this paperwork has a "home" where it can be easily stored, it is less likely to be lost or ruined.

You will need to purchase for the "Stay-At-Home" Missionary Journals:

- Two 2" wide, sturdy "view" binders for keeping all the missionary's letters, pictures, and vital documents. Label the front, back, and spines "Stay-At-Home Missionary Journal" or label them with your missionary's name and mission.

- 50 or so sheets of archival heavy-duty 110# cardstock upon which to mount the pictures and mementos that are sent home.

- About 50 high quality, archival sheet protectors to protect the treasures. Non-glare, heavy-duty sheet protectors are preferred because these "journals" need to last a long time.

- One or two boxes of ¼" archival quality scrapbook mounting squares (sticky on both sides for easy use).

- Several archival marking pens for making notes under pictures and paperwork that the missionary may send home and are then kept in the

"Stay-At-Home" Missionary Journals. It is best to list the location, the complete date, and the first *and* last names of all the people in each picture. Memories fade quickly and the information may be more difficult to recover later.

See page 205 for more details about what to keep in the "Stay-At-Home" Missionary Journals.

❑ "Missionary Affairs" Binder.

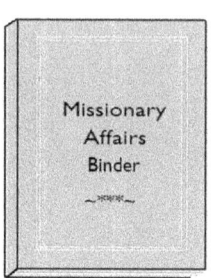

While your missionary is away, keep accurate financial records, prepare their tax returns, and store other information and paperwork in an organized manner. This will make everyone's life easier. To facilitate this, you will need to gather or purchase:

- One 2" view binder that is labeled front, back and down the spine "Missionary Affairs."

- Five or more binder tab dividers. These can be labeled:
    - ❑ Finances
    - ❑ Taxes
    - ❑ Usernames and Passwords
    - ❑ Contact Information
    - ❑ Instructions (College admissions, housing, jobs, etc.)

During the mission tenure, keep bank statements, withdrawal and deposit paperwork, and other personal financial information for the missionary in an organized manner behind the "Finances" tab. You may also decide to keep a list of your missionary's active bank accounts, any necessary access information for internet banking, and their specific instructions on how to proceed when CDs mature or funds need transferring.

Behind the "Taxes" tab, keep the necessary information to fill out the tax returns for your son or daughter during their absence. This location will also be where you can keep copies of their tax returns. When your missionary returns, the "Missionary Affairs" Binder can be passed on to him or her.

Your missionary likely has several usernames and passwords (and often email addresses) that should be in a trusted person's possession to facilitate handling their affairs while they are absent. This may be your specific responsibility, in which case you would keep this information behind the "Usernames and Passwords" tab in the "Missionary Affairs" Binder. Should your missionary choose someone else, make sure this person's contact information is detailed behind the "Contact Information" tab in the "Missionary Affairs" Binder.

See "Finances" on page 207 for more details about the use of the "Missionary Affairs" Binder.

❏ "Mission Preparations" Wall Calendar.

Purchase or find one large, wall calendar and mount it on a convenient surface to quickly notate and visually remember missionary preparations. This helps appropriate family members fulfill their obligations as the weeks pass and gives you a larger, visual picture of just how long it is before the big day, especially if you mark in red the number of days until your missionary's departure on each calendar square.

You may also indicate each person's responsibilities using a different colored pen. This can act as a gentle hint to everyone involved.

Keep track of the many preparation details on both the smaller "Mission Preparations" Binder calendars (with the addition of your personal notes and written goals) and the "Mission Preparations" Wall Calendar (as a public reminder).

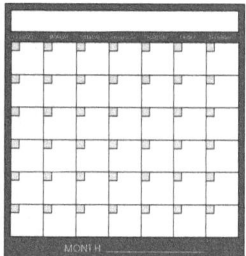

In addition to marking the departure date, note when certain items need to be done, when you, your spouse, and/or your missionary are to have commitments completed, when passport information is to be prepared and mailed, when it is due back to you, when doctor's follow-up appointments are to be kept, when shots are being given (as some immunizations are administered in a series with some time between each), and all the other sundries which are part of the missionary's preparations. This will allow pacing to be planned, obligations to be met, and stress levels to stay at a manageable level.

Also note important dates on the calendars:

- Date, time, and place when your missionary plans to get his or her endowment. (This should be done as soon as possible to allow for continued spiritual preparation.)

- Possible dates when you and your missionary will be returning to the temple together.

- Date when you will have a formal family picture taken (should you choose to do this).

- Date for the sacrament meeting talk.

- Date to be set apart by stake or district president (which date usually happens the week of).

- Date of departure.

In other words, as you plan and prepare, write it down, *write it down!*

❑ Stationery, Address Labels, and Stamps.

In addition to the regular emails you may send, consider purchasing enough stationery supplies to facilitate occasional letter writing while the missionary is in the Missionary Training Center. The stationery would best be 8.5" x 11" in size and three-hole punched so that after your letters are read, they can easily be saved by the missionary in a binder.

Purchase and/or prepare address labels and adhere them to the envelopes. This makes writing and sending letters more convenient and gives the missionary tangible correspondence to treasure and re-read as desired.

It might delight and comfort your missionary if a letter is waiting for him or her upon their arrival at the Missionary Training Center. This is especially helpful if your missionary is going to an overseas Missionary Training Center. Another approach is to tuck a letter in their luggage to find when they are unpacking!

Note on the yearly calendars in the "Missionary Preparations" Binder the dates you will be writing a letter or email while your missionary is in the Missionary Training Center. This will help you get into a writing routine until this habit is firmly established. A regular letter from home is manna to a lonely, stressed, and sometimes-homesick missionary.

❑ File Clerk Decision.

Decide right up front who will be the "file clerk" to keep track of the many documents that are part of a missionary's preparations.

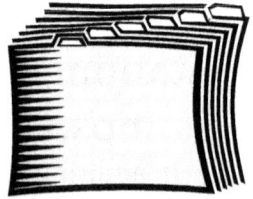

In some homes, the mother takes care of these responsibilities: Collecting all documentation as the mission preparations take place, keeping up this function as emails to and from the missionary are printed and stored, mounting photographs as they are received, and keeping the whole mission experience orderly and retrievable upon demand.

In other homes, the missionary desires to keep this particular part of the mission to him or herself before they leave and then passes the stewardship on at their departure. Either way, it is important to know up front who will keep track of this paperwork!

Having said this, I found it was best for one of the parents to keep an extra *copy of every important document so should anything get lost, misplaced, or otherwise disappear while in another's stewardship, a copy is convenient so the mission can still happen.*

❏ Physical and Dental Exam Appointments.

Make an appointment with your son or daughter's physician and your dentist for any follow-up medical and/or dental needs which may be outstanding.

One of our sons went for his pre-mission physical and was told he needed some minor skin surgery before his departure. This meant another trip, this time to a specialist. The trauma of outpatient surgery took vital energy and time from a tight schedule. If I were to do it again, any follow-up physical exams and dental visits would take higher priority in our list of preparations.

This experience and others have taught me that complications in mission preparations come from many directions. Therefore, being early wherever and however you can will make things easier all the way around. So call and make these dental and physical exam appointments right away.

Your dentist may be booked, your missionary might also need to have other dental work done (and find a good weekend for this recovery), or your missionary might need additional medical treatments that will take precious time from a packed schedule. Starting early with dentists and doctors really helps keep the preparations moving forward in a timely manner!

Missionary (often with the aid of one or both parents) –

> *"And they fasted much and prayed much that the Lord would grant unto them a portion of his Spirit to go with them, and abide with them, that they might be an instrument in the hands of God."* Alma 17:9

The initial surprise and excitement should give way quickly to extensive preparations, all of which will make a tremendous difference during the first few weeks and months of the actual mission field experience. Therefore, this section of the book is written directly to the missionary. Remember to always counsel with the Lord as you make personal mission preparations and then consider doing the following items as soon as possible.

❏ The Missionary Packet.

Review the Missionary Packet very carefully. A lot won't seem important or relevant the first time through, so plan to read it again in about a week and then again in another month. Questions you will have as you prepare for your mission are usually answered in the packet; you just didn't notice them before. Re-reading alleviates stress, helps re-orient your activities, and aids in making "to do" lists as you continue your mission preparations.

❏ Patriarchal Blessing and Temple Endowment.

Although a patriarchal blessing is often given before a mission call, it is a requirement for mission preparations. In addition, a temple recommend interview should be planned for almost *immediately* by speaking with your bishop or branch president.

Often a missionary will serve where temple attendance will happen infrequently, if at all. If possible, get the endowment early and return to the temple as often as possible. Do whatever else your local leaders advise to prepare spiritually for your upcoming mission.

❑ Mission Internet Site.

Find your mission's internet site, if there is one. Review it thoroughly, especially to find returned missionaries that might be living near you or are available by email. Asking questions and getting answers from previous missionaries is invaluable as you prepare. While you must balance what they say with the directions you will receive in your Missionary Packet and from your mission president directly, it clarifies your anticipated experiences and makes preparations easier.

❑ Foreign Language Preparations.

If you will be speaking a foreign language, listen to enough of the new language (on the internet or by speaking to returned missionaries) to be able to recognize it, and then continue (as much as possible) to familiarize yourself with the swing of the jargon and the sounds of words, phrases, and sentences.

While all the language preparation you can get will be invaluable, don't be surprised if after initial interest, you can't bear the thought of learning much more about the language until you begin your mission. Getting ready for a mission takes a lot of emotional energy and occasionally some things have to wait until you are more prepared. You will learn more, much more, in the Missionary Training Center.

❑ Mission Preparation Supplies.

As you begin to officially prepare for your mission, there are several items to immediately gather or purchase. They include:

- An 8.5" x 11" clipboard to contain your written lists and keep them readily available as ideas come to you.

- Storage boxes. These are sturdy boxes available at your nearby copy center or office supply store. If you purchase flattened "banker's" boxes, put them and their lids together so you can begin packing personal belongings. You will use these boxes to sort, pack, and separate items you plan to share with others. Also, find or purchase packing materials to use as needed!

- Permanent Marking Pen. It is important to liberally label the boxes you will be packing. Label the top and *both* ends of each box to facilitate easy retrieval of your belongings. Writing in large letters makes your labeling easier to read!

- Packing Tape. Have packing tape readily available so when a box is full and ready to store, you can tape it up securely, label it easily, and set is aside. One more thing done!

- Part of your mission preparations will include making some difficult and sometimes tedious decisions. A clipboard and several lists will facilitate deciding what to do with this and that, where to put this and that, and how to wrap up this and that in your life. So collect these supplies and begin making plans. This will propel you into purposeful action and steady accomplishment.

❏ "Items to Take" List.

Begin with a preliminary written list entitled "<u>Items to Take</u>" (on your mission). Choose one place, preferably a sturdy box, to gather items you "want to take" so when you find or purchase them during the next few weeks, they will have a safe "home" as you prepare for your mission.

❑ "Items to Discard" List.

Begin a second written list entitled "<u>Items to Discard</u>" as you will most likely need to go through your personal items and make some important decisions.

Also, label a box or container "Items to Discard" so you will have a place to put these items when you begin sorting.

❑ "Items to Pack and Store" List.

Begin a third list entitled "<u>Items to Pack and Store</u>" for those items going into storage before you leave. Make special note of those items that are particularly important to you and need careful handling and packing to endure two years of storage.

Then begin putting items in the storage boxes you have gathered or purchased. Pack carefully and tightly, adding packing material as needed. When a box is full, taped, and labeled three times, set it aside.

Most of the time, it turns out best to carefully pack and put into sturdy boxes all those items you want to have in good condition upon your return.

Anything you leave out can and probably will be somewhat more "used" upon your homecoming. If you really care about it, pack it away!

❏ "Items to Share" List.

Make a fourth written list entitled "Items to Share" with your siblings, friends, or extended family. Usually these are useable items you have outgrown, out-loved, or just don't need any more.

As before, label a box or container for keeping these items as you gather them and (when convenient) begin to share these items with friends and family. Don't keep much of anything you have outgrown, no longer love, or don't think you will ever use again. Sharing before a mission is very liberating to body and soul! It also endears you to siblings, other family members, and important friends.

❏ "Projects to Finish & Put Away" List.

Entitle a fifth list of "Projects to Finish and Put Away" for the time being. Two years or even eighteen months is a long time to leave anything dangling or without attention. Things will likely not be the same when you return, so bring your life "to a stopping point" (as much as possible) so you can enter the mission field without distracting, outstanding items or issues.

Because forgetting is so easy with an eighteen-month to two-year absence, it is best to make written notes to yourself about what you decide, how you left things, and how to being again. Then, when you return, you can start up with confidence and less confusion.

One of our sons was in the middle of writing a book when his mission call came. He made notes to himself about where his computer files were located, made backups of his work on a labeled CD, and otherwise brought this project to a place of closure and safety while he was gone. This proved providential, as he successfully started right up again on this project soon after his arrival home.

If you are attending a vocational school or university on scholarship, it will likely be necessary to defer your scholarship during your absence. This takes some phone calls, an email, or even a visit to the scholarship office, probably filling out the necessary paperwork, and giving your parents written instructions on how to activate the scholarship at the appropriate time so it will be available upon your return.

It is also possible you will have a relationship that might need putting on hold. Make sure you are adequately verbal about your feelings and intentions so no misunderstandings linger after your departure. Even then, know that sometimes "Dear John" or "Dear Jane" letters might be received while serving your mission.

❑ "Financial and Other Arrangements to Make" List.

Entitle a sixth list "<u>Financial and Other Arrangements to Make</u>." This includes appointing someone to be your "power of attorney" while you are absent and getting the necessary paperwork completed and notarized. This person can act in your behalf and make financial arrangements, register you for school, and otherwise handle your affairs while you are away.

Another way to address this need is to ask the appropriate institutions what will be needed for your parents to act in your behalf. With schools this often means a particular kind of letter of consent; with banks it might mean adding one of the parent's names to your accounts.

Because of the new medical privacy laws, it may be necessary for you to sign releases for your parents, or another trusted individual, to have access to your medical records, especially if you are going out of the country. This paperwork is usually included in the Missionary Packet.

Of course, before you leave on your mission, all outstanding debts need to be resolved. Listing these and any other outstanding issues on your list will facilitate getting them off your mind as you proceed towards final preparations.

❑ "Usernames and Passwords" List.

Someone trustworthy will need to know the usernames, passwords (and sometimes email addresses) of your life. Often this person will be your father or mother, but wisely choose someone you can completely trust. Prepare a "Usernames and Passwords" list so this written information can be kept safe. Include instructions on how and when you desire this information to be used.

Some higher education facilities require a username and password to access grades, register for classes, and pay tuition online.

Name_____

	Internet site	User name	Email address	Password	Date
1					
2					
3					
4					
5					
6					
7					
8					
9					
10					
11					
12					
13					
14					
15					
16					
17					
18					
19					
20					

If you do your banking and bill paying online, the appropriate usernames and passwords will also be helpful to anyone taking care of your finances during your absence.

Have someone check your email account for a while. They will need access to your account, including your email address and password, to successfully take care of this item for you.

The "Usernames and Passwords" List on page 28 can be downloaded and printed for your personal use at *http://houseoforder.com/category/downloads/*.

❏ Stuffing Doesn't Work.

Sometimes missionaries feel like they have to "stuff" the last few days and weeks of their pre-mission time with lots of fun activities, marginal events, and otherwise really good times before they enter the "doom" of missionary service. This doesn't help much, because on the first day at the Missionary Training Center you will realize there is much work to be done for the Lord and you might have prepared otherwise. On the other hand, moving towards missionary routines, shifting your priorities to pondering and appreciating the Gospel does help because you come to the Missionary Training Center focused and ready. It makes a tremendous difference and it is the better decision!

❏ Writing Materials.

Stationery, stamps, and envelopes for your use can be purchased along with many of your other needs and packed in the Office Kit. See "Preparations of Essential Kits" on page 128 for more details.

As you begin your mission preparations, other action items may occur to you. Keeping written lists will offset the increased stress as the important day approaches and keep you on track even when your brain stops working so well!

Siblings, Extended Family, and Friends –

> *"I hope that our young men, and our young women, will rise to the challenge... We must raise the bar on the worthiness and qualifications of those who go into the world as ambassadors of the Lord Jesus Christ."* Gordon B. Hinckley, Nov. 2002 *Ensign*, pg. 57

Siblings, extended family members, and friends can be especially helpful during mission preparation times. They can relieve stress for the parents and missionary plus strengthen family bonds and friendships by participating in preparatory activities even as they meet their own emotional needs.

❑ **Special Activity.**
Choose one last special activity to do with the missionary. It doesn't need to be extravagant or elaborate, but it does need to be meaningful.

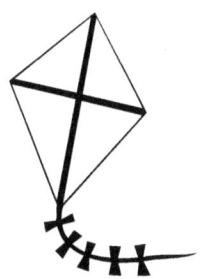

❑ **Pictures.**
Have a picture taken of yourself and the missionary for posting in a convenient place while they are gone.

❑ **Writing Materials.**
Decide now to write the missionary regularly. He or she will need your support, your confidence, and your letters telling of your positive experiences, your feelings for the Gospel, and your testimony.

Purchase enough stationery and envelopes to write regular letters while the missionary is in the Missionary Training Center. A written letter is greatly treasured by those working for the Lord!

Prepare address labels, return address labels, and stamps. Adhere them to the envelopes to make sending letters convenient and easy.

Plan a regular time to write your letters so the missionary can anticipate hearing from you from time to time while in the Missionary Training Center. If you desire, purchase more stationery supplies and continue writing letters as part of your weekly or monthly routine during their extended absence. A regular, encouraging letter is like a good dessert to a missionary. Can't get enough of it!

"Treasure up wisdom...If ye are prepared, ye shall not fear." D&C 38:30

When the Mission Call Comes, Go To Work Checklist

Dad –
- ☐ Missionary Packet.
- ☐ Finances.
- ☐ Wall Map.

Mom –
- ☐ Worry List.
- ☐ Missionary Packet.
- ☐ Calendar Calculation.
- ☐ Stash Shelf.
- ☐ Shot Records.
- ☐ Thank You Supplies.
- ☐ Mission Announcement Letter.
- ☐ "Mission Preparations" Binder.
    - One 2" view binder
    - Five+ tabbed dividers
    - Binder pencil holder
    - Pens and pencils
    - Lined paper
    - Sheet protectors
    - Cardstock
    - Monthly calendars
    - Yearly calendars
- ☐ Sentimental Activities List.
- ☐ "Stay-At-Home" Missionary Journals
    - Two 2" view binders
    - 50+ sheets cardstock

Organize for a Mission

When the Mission Call Comes, Go To Work Checklist
(continued)

- 50+ sheet protectors
- Scrapbook mounting squares
- Scrapbook pens

☐ "Missionary Affairs" Binder.
- One 2" view binder
- Five+ tabbed dividers

☐ "Missionary Affairs" Wall Calendar.
☐ Stationery, Address Labels, and Stamps.
☐ File Clerk Decision.
☐ Physical/Dental Exam Appointments.

Missionary –

☐ Missionary Packet.
☐ Patriarchal Blessing and Temple Endowment.
☐ Mission Internet Site.
☐ Foreign Language Preparations.
☐ Mission Preparation Supplies.
- Clipboard
- Storage boxes
- Packing materials
- Permanent marking pen
- Packing tape

☐ "Items to Take" List.
☐ "Items to Discard" List.

When the Mission Call Comes, Go To Work Checklist
(continued)

- ☐ "Items to Pack and Store" List.
- ☐ "Items to Share" List.
- ☐ "Projects to Finish and Put Away" List.
- ☐ "Financial and Other Arrangements to Make" List.
- ☐ "Usernames and Passwords" List.
- ☐ See "Office Kit" under "Preparation of Essential Kits" on page 132 for information about stationery, envelopes, and postage for the missionary's use.

Siblings, Extended Family, & Friends –

- ☐ Special Activity.
- ☐ Pictures.
- ☐ Writing Materials.
  - Stationery and envelopes
  - Address labels
  - Return address labels

- ☐ Stamps.

Items to Buy and Take

"Do not run faster or labor more than you have strength and means provided...but be diligent unto the end... Pray always, that you may come off conqueror." D&C 10:4-5

It is useful to prepare a written list of all items that need to be purchased, how many of each item your missionary will need, the anticipated cost per item, and the potential total cost for all purchases. The total possible expenditure is usually a surprise, but knowing how expensive it might be helps keep the total possible outlay in mind. It might even aid in keeping the amounts spent somewhat under control.

This initial shopping list and written budget facilitates all future shopping. Extensive shopping will yield good choices, higher quality, and the best possible prices. Don't be too anxious to get it "now" if you don't feel it is the best choice. Being organized often means shopping longer!

An example "Items to Buy and Take" form is printed on page 38. This form is also available for downloading at *http://houseoforder.com/category/downloads/*. Again, this book is a guide of what to look for once you know what you need and want to buy. It can help you make wiser, more informed choices.

This chapter is divided into several sections for convenience in making your lists:

> 1) Items to Buy and Take – Bigger Investments, page 39.
>
> 2) Items to Buy and Take – Clothing for Elders and Sisters, page 52.
>
> 3) Items to Buy and Take – Clothing Specifically for Elders, page 65.
>
> 4) Items to Buy and Take – Clothing Specifically for Sisters, page 84.
>
> 5) Items to Buy and Take – Additional Useful Items, page 104.

Organize for a Mission

Item	Details	Number to Buy	Budget Each	Budget Total	Places to Shop

Items to Buy and Take – Bigger Investments

"Therefore, be ye... wise... and I will order all things for your good." D&C 111:11

When shopping for missionary supplies, there are some big-ticket items to purchase. Shop for these items with care because of their greater cost and the heightened need for good quality.

Understandably, not every item will be appropriate for your missionary's particular area of service. For your convenience, these "Items to Buy and Take" are listed in alphabetical order to facilitate finding information as quickly and easily as possible.

❏ Bicycle.

Some missions require a bike. This can be purchased before the missionary leaves and the bike can be shipped to the mission. Or, it might be purchased when the missionary is in the field. However it happens, it is important that funds are available to the missionary to make these arrangements.

Before the mission, visit a bike store with the missionary, talk to a knowledgeable clerk, and learn what to look for when buying a bike, especially if the missionary will be making this decision while in the mission field. Brakes, gears, tires, tube protectors, frame, weight, and style are important considerations.

Bicycle accessories, such as a lock and a bike helmet, may also be needed. These requirements vary from mission to mission. Whether purchased before the missionary leaves and shipped or acquired later in the field, these items will take additional funds from the mission preparations budget.

❏ Books.

Several books are allowed in the mission field. They can come from the missionary's own library or be purchased as desired. They include:

- ❏ *True To The Faith*
- ❏ *Jesus the Christ*
- ❏ *Our Heritage: A Brief History of The Church of Jesus Christ of Latter-day Saints*
- ❏ *Our Search for Happiness*

If someone asks, these are wonderful gifts to receive from family and friends.

Because your missionary will be accumulating some eight to twelve pounds of literature in the Missionary Training Center, consider the additional weight involved when deciding to take Church books on the mission. They add significant heaviness to any suitcase.

❏ Camera.

Follow the counsel to spend less on a camera. It can get lost, stolen, and otherwise prejudice the local people against the missionary if it is too expensive or elaborate. If it shoots high-quality pictures and it is easy to use, it should be sufficient for mission memories.

When purchasing a digital camera, acquire an adequate-sized memory card or two. Store the second memory card in the Spares Kit (see page 141).

In addition, consider the best way to back-up memory cards so priceless photo computer files remain safe. Also, buy one or more backup sets of camera batteries and keep in the Spares Kit (see page 141).

One of my son's missionary companions used a digital camera and stored all his pictures on one memory card that failed him in the last weeks of his mission. He lost all the pictures from 22 months of serving. Whatever method is used for storing photos, making a backup on a separate memory device or sending the digital photo files home, as part of week-to-week emails, is an essential part of any photo memory plan!

❑ Eyeglasses or Contacts.

For the missionary who wears eyeglasses, it would be wise to have a second pair. This may entail a purchase and then careful packing of this second pair for future use. A contacts back-up plan should also be implemented.

In addition, a copy of the latest eyeglasses/contacts prescription should be sent with the missionary into the field for accurately replacing eyewear as needed.

❏ Journals, Daily (at least two, maybe three).

Daily journals need to last through the mission, including travel during transfers, writing in them daily, and then a lifetime past that. Find ones with good quality covers, sturdy bindings, and high-quality, archival paper.

This is one place to spend generously. Send enough journals to last two years so they will be consistent in size, shape, and quality. After purchasing, enter the missionary's name, contact information, and home address so in the event they are lost or stolen, they have a chance of being returned.

One of our sons was a more prolific writer and filled two journals and had begun a third before he came home. Because we only sent him with two journals, the third one is smaller and of poorer quality, but was the best he could find where he was serving at the time. Our other three sons filled only about one and three-quarters journals, so judge according to your missionary writing style and prolificacy!

A Sister shares: "I kept a daily journal which I really treasure. I wrote in it almost every night before I went to bed and glued in pictures, bus pass stubs, and museum pamphlets that I can look at now and remember.

"I also had a little calendar I kept at the end of my mission that I wish I had kept the whole time. At the end of the day my companion and I would write down highlights of the day on

this calendar. At the end of the transfer we would go back and read about each of the days and remember how the Lord had blessed us. It was awesome!"

❏ Journal(s), Study.

Sturdy, mid-sized bound "study" journals are invaluable for making notes as the missionary studies each morning during his or her mission in conjunction with *Preach My Gospel*. These journals should be somewhat different in style and color than the daily journals for ease in locating them amongst personal items.

A Sister shares: "Bring a study journal and use it. I found a great system that worked for me. I had a journal that had numbered pages. When I would study one of the sections in Preach My Gospel, *I often would write next to it the page number where I had written notes about that section in my study journal. It made it easy to find when I wanted to read my notes on that topic, as well as let me know if I had studied that section already or not."*

❏ Luggage.

Of all the purchases that are made, luggage tends to be rather important because it holds, carries, and often stores the missionary's personal belongings. Therefore, shop and spend carefully on luggage, always looking for the best quality and the most appealing features.

There are several important characteristics to look for when purchasing luggage. They include:

"Piggyback" Luggage. Pieces of luggage that attach to each other via "piggy backing" make independence much easier while traveling. Make sure the clipping mechanisms work well, don't separate easily, and are convenient to use. Remember, even with the convenience of sturdy luggage that attaches together, tackling stairs may mean several trips up and down as pieces are detached, moved, and then reattached together.

Handles. All handles should be securely attached to the luggage. Pull-out handles (the kind that retract into the luggage when not in use) are usually better constructed if there is a push button to release the mechanism versus the "pull on it hard enough" action that sometimes leads to the handle coming completely apart from the suitcase.

Zippers. Zippers especially need to be wide, thick, and well built. They should work easily when opening and closing. Check the zippers on all pieces of luggage to avoid a poorly sewn zipper that gets caught from the beginning or one that does not run back and forth effortlessly.

A second exterior zipper on suitcases that allows them to "expand" with an additional inch or two of depth will make for easier traveling both to and during the mission experience, as packing won't need to be done quite so tightly.

Occasionally there will be an additional interior zipper around the luggage lid that allows a suit to be carefully packed separate from the rest of the missionary's belongings. This facilitates suits staying pressed and looking great right out of the suitcase.

<u>Wheels</u>. Wheels should be on every possible piece of luggage. They should be larger versus smaller, and work well when running on slick floors, bumpy cobbles, and commercial carpet. Some higher quality luggage will have four roller blade-type wheels with ball bearings, a plus when lugging a lot of weight. The missionary will move luggage frequently. Make sure everything works well!

Roll the largest piece of luggage (with all the smaller pieces inside to add weight) around at the store both on areas with carpet and hard flooring to get a feel of the durability of the wheels. Next, attach the various pieces of luggage together and try manhandling it alone. Do the wheels still work well? Can the luggage be moved without additional help?

<u>Sturdy Corners and Stress Points</u>. Because missionary luggage gets a lot of abuse, strengthening at the corners and other stress points will help the pieces last longer. Pieces of luggage that nestle neatly inside each other have a wonderful storage convenience.

<u>Lining</u>. The suitcase lining should be well secured at the edges. Sometimes you can find a lining that zips open to allow access to the handle mechanism which is a plus if the handle gets stuck in the "out" position or refuses to release. A heavier lining fabric with a tighter weave offers more durability.

<u>Kick Plate</u>. Some higher quality luggage, especially on the two larger pieces, has a kick plate on the rear

between the wheels. This is one place that is often knocked with a missionary's shoe to tip the luggage in preparation for moving it. The kick plate keeps the luggage from becoming dented, punctured, and eventually broken in that area.

<u>Feet</u>. Look for rubber "feet" on the sides and bottom of the luggage that will allow it to rest slightly above the floor without the actual suitcase touching the floor. This will keep interior contents from moisture and dirt whenever the luggage is stored, moved, or transported.

<u>Accessories</u>. Additional accessories that often come with luggage are usually unnecessary and rarely used during missionary service. For this reason, if it doesn't seem to be helpful, don't buy it; and, if it comes with the set, leave it home!

Although darker luggage tends to stay clean looking the longest, a different color (and maybe even luggage with a bit of pattern) will make it easier to find personal suitcases amongst the many other pieces when traveling and during transfers. Of the entire room of luggage I saw at the Missionary Training Center when one of my sons departed, I only saw one set of red in the enormous sea of black, brown, and navy suitcases. That missionary had an easier time at every transfer, every airport, and with every bus he or she took.

<u>Locks</u>. Consider carefully before buying luggage with built-in locks. If these locks fail or the keys are lost, the luggage cannot easily be opened or used again.

Items to Buy and Take

<u>Labeling</u>. Label each piece of luggage carefully, creatively, and in plain sight to make suitcases easier to retrieve at airports, during transfers, at bus depots, and when unloading from vehicles. The addition of colorful strips of fabric, bright pieces of string, and other easy-to-recognize identifiers make traveling that much easier.

A Sister who served in South America advises: "I bought one large suitcase, one small suitcase, and a medium-sized duffel for my luggage. I wish I had bought two large suitcases and one small suitcase and foregone the duffel as it could hold practically nothing, and Sisters need all the space they can get.

"I didn't realize two larger suitcases were okay by mission standards. And even though it is hard to move around in the airport or bus terminal (in the field between transfers) with three suitcases, it can be done and would have made my life easier. You can also "piggyback" the smaller suitcase to one of the larger suitcases and pull these pieces of luggage with two hands.

"One day of luggage hassle on transfer day is worth the extra space."

❏ Music CD Player.

Listening to music is allowed in the mission field with certain restrictions. Check with the mission's specific rules before making a purchase or packing an audio player. In general, these players should be simple, hand-held styles with speakers. Earphones and video music players are not allowed.

A Sister shares: "Music is VERY important for me and it was very hard for me to not have music in my life. After a few months in the field, I purchased an audio player and small computer speakers and listened to inspirational music in the morning as we ate breakfast or at night when we got home after a long day. To those that have music as a big part of their life or who are moved spiritually by music, I would definitely recommend having this capacity while on a mission."

❏ Razor.

Because being "clean shaven" is essential to missionary work, each Elder will need a good razor that can be easily used to meet daily "missionary grooming" needs. It need not be fancy, but should be in good working order. The same advice goes to meet Sister's grooming needs.

One of our sons said an interesting first day at the Missionary Training Center included a bathroom wastebasket full of bloodied tissues left by missionaries who were not well versed in using shaving cream and a straight edge razor, their chosen way of shaving at the Missionary Training Center.

❏ Scriptures.

Missionaries will need a set of scriptures in their native language. These need not be expensive but should be durable because they will get well used, be well read, and become well marked over the duration of the mission.

Scriptures from seminary or teenage experience can be used or a new set purchased, as the missionary will be studying with new perspectives, focused training, and added spiritual insights. Either way, personal scriptures let a missionary notate from the special point of view mission experiences bring.

If going to a mission with a foreign language, scriptures in that language are usually acquired as part of the Missionary Training Center experience.

❑ Watch.

Spend less on a watch. If it tells time and can act as an alarm clock, it is enough.
Watches get lost, stolen, and otherwise bias the local people against missionaries if they are expensive or showy.

Spare watch batteries should be purchased and put in the Spares Kit (see page 141).

A Sister who served in South America shares, "I bought a cheap watch at a local store to wear during my mission. I think it cost $10-15 dollars. It had a velcro wristband. I didn't want a nice watch to be tempting to thieves on the street."

One of our sons had his watch suddenly torn from his wrist while waiting at a bus stop at the beginning of his mission. The watch was replaceable, as he bought another soon after, but it was an emotional loss, which helped him realize that much of what he owned might not make it through the mission.

> *This lesson helped our other missionaries desire to take "tools" instead of "treasures" during their missionary labors. In other words, don't take what you can and will probably lose, have ruined, or wear out. Leave it home if it matters a great deal to you!*

As you shop, consider, and then purchase these larger investments for the mission, remember to buy quality long enough to last the term of the mission, quantity enough to allow for mishaps, and maybe have an extra sum of money set aside for any replacements that may be necessary.

Items to Buy and Take – Bigger Investments Checklist

- ❏ Bicycle.
- ❏ Books.
  - *True To The Faith*
  - *Jesus the Christ*
  - *Our Heritage: A Brief History of The Church of Jesus Christ of Latter-day Saints*
  - *Our Search for Happiness*

- ❏ Camera.
- ❏ Eyeglasses or Contacts.
- ❏ Journals, Daily.
- ❏ Journal(s), Study.
- ❏ Luggage.
- ❏ Music CD Player.
- ❏ Razor.
- ❏ Scriptures.
- ❏ Watch.

Items to Buy and Take – Clothing For Elders and Sisters

"And took nothing with him save it were his ...provisions." 1 Nephi 2:4

When purchasing clothing items for a mission, four characteristics must be considered: fabric type, fabric durability, fit, and quality of construction. Don't be in such a hurry that you buy without carefully checking each item of clothing and accessory thoroughly for ample fit, appropriate fabric type and durability, and quality of construction including seams, buttons, zippers, and hemming. You will also want to consider how easy each clothing item will be to maintain and clean.

As before, this list is in alphabetical order to make accessing information easier. Remember, all items will not be needed by every missionary. Use the following information to make the best decisions for each missionary's particular situation.

❑ Belts.
When choosing belts, consider that leather will usually last longer than vinyl, as it tends not to split, especially at the buckle. Always spend just a bit more so the missionary can plan on eighteen months to two good year's use without worry.

❑ Earmuffs.
Of course, earmuffs are only for the missionary going to a colder area and would be worn only with the approval of the mission president. While there are many different kinds, the least conspicuous ones

wrap around the back of the neck. They are less noticeable, convenient to store in pockets, and nicely keep out the cold air.

❑ Flip-flops.

Many missionaries are asked to bring a pair of flip-flops (sometimes referred to as sandals) to keep their feet from touching shower floors (and in some missions, any floors at all). Choose two pairs that are sturdy, flexible, and comfortable. Use the first pair for showering. The second pair makes it possible to have "dry" flip flops to wear around the abode to let feet "air out," to have a change from walking shoes, and to feel "comfortable" at the end of the day.

❑ Garments.

Because garments are very personal, they must be chosen with care. In addition, make sure there are more garments sent on the mission than there are days in the week.

Without realizing it, one of our sons took ONLY seven pairs of garments and either wore a pair twice a week or hand-washed one pair in the middle of each week (which wasn't convenient for him). As parents, we didn't learn about this situation until he came home.

Crew neck style and/or thermal garments are much warmer than those of a lighter fabric, so they are more useful in cooler seasons. Keep to the lower neck style for warmer seasons. Everything that can be done to be comfortable will be helpful on long missionary days!

Because this is a very personal decision, I found it best to let our pre-missionaries choose three different garment styles, sizes, and/or fabrics to try out for a week or two after their first trip to the temple. It soon became apparent (especially after several washes and wearings) which garments seem most suited to each individual. It was only then that we bought garments in bulk.

❑ Gloves.

Again, gloves are for those going to colder climates. There are many different kinds of gloves with many qualities, but layering seems to offer the best option for keeping hands warm in very cold weather. Thin gloves are worn underneath. Larger, heavier wool gloves go on the outside. Try on different varieties, but know that just because it says it will keep your hands warm on the label, doesn't guarantee very much. Buy what will work for you!

As a Sister explains about her cold winter European mission experience: "I wouldn't advise getting mittens. You will be using your hands so much on the streets when you are contacting people and writing their phone numbers down, you want to be able to use your fingers.

"Wool is a must; whatever you can find that has wool in it, buy it. Wool socks, wool gloves, woolen scarves and hats are also a necessity."

Remember, all woolen clothing items will need to be protected from potential damage by moths. This is easily done with small pieces of cedar wood placed in and around the items when they are stored in suitcase, closets, or cupboards.

❑ Gym Clothes.

See entries under "Clothing Specifically for Elders" on page 65 and "Clothing Specifically for Sisters" on page 84.

❑ Handkerchiefs.

Yes, handkerchiefs are useful for clearing off sweat, wiping and blowing, and are helpful for both Elders and Sisters. Facial tissue is nice, but it can't be washed, dried and reused, something handkerchiefs excel at every day of the mission.

Buy white, usually one dozen, large handkerchiefs. These are handy tools in any missionary's pocket and can be useful in so many ways.

Using a handkerchief increases the chances of using proper etiquette according to the local customs, especially those of foreign countries (instead of wiping a runny nose on a sleeve, pulling perspiration off the forehead with a credit card, or discarding used facial tissue inappropriately).

❑ Outerwear, Overcoat.

If requested in the Missionary Packet, buy an overcoat to best suit the year-round weather conditions of the locality where the missionary will serve. First, investigate the probable temperature ranges and types of weather where he or she will be serving. Then learn from others what kind of overcoat would be best for the mission.

In colder areas, a heavy-duty, full-length, lined overcoat will make each and every miserable weather day just a little nicer. The overcoat needs to have "substance," meaning it will be heavier and thicker, which will help keep the cold and wet out even as it keeps the warmth and dryness in. Avoid coats which look and feel "flimsy."

In the clothing industry, overcoats are usually sized the same as a suit. So if an Elder wears a size 42 suit jacket, he would wear a size 42 overcoat. Sisters can best find an overcoat by trying them on.

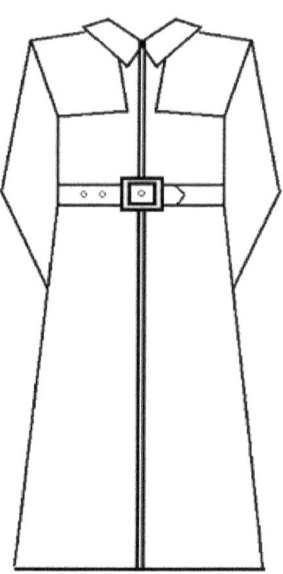

Because this is an individual decision, put on a suit before trying on overcoats to make sure there is enough "space" to move about freely.

In addition, if going to an especially cold mission, put on both a sweater and a suit jacket before trying on overcoats to make sure there is ample room for comfort.

It is useful if the overcoat is longer than shorter (to keep the rain and snow off legs), larger than smaller (to allow for layering underneath), and can be buttoned up (or cinched) at the neck, sleeves and waist as this cinching also keeps the cold air out and body heat in.

Large, deep pockets are essential for holding accessories like gloves, earmuffs, and scarves. An additional interior pocket is useful for keeping important items both secure and dry.

A detachable woolen collar will add warmth and a detachable hood is especially useful for Sisters and gives them additional options and protection on cold and windy days.

A woolen lining gives substantial warmth to an overcoat as it keeps the cold out and the body heat in even as it breathes. Look for linings with about 70% wool content. It is best if the lining is almost as long as the coat to add warmth not only to the core of the body but also to the legs. The lining should be removable to allow use of the outerwear on milder days. A zip-out lining is nicer than a buttoned one because it saves precious time when removing or inserting the lining. A better quality overcoat will also have a second, lightweight, sewn-in lining to allow for ease of movement when only the shell of the overcoat is worn.

Some woolen linings are quilted across the shoulder area with the addition of a slick fabric. This allows for additional warmth and ease of movement within the overcoat.

Some overcoats come with a cape across the back yoke and at the front on each shoulder. This is called the European trench coat and has the advantage of shedding water away from the body at the places where most of the rain and snow falls, especially across the back. The moisture falls, runs down these outside yokes, and falls away to the ground.

Look for extra buttons that are usually attached to the coat inside the front seam. These will make it easy to replace a button should one become lost. They can either be left sewn on the coat or kept in the "Sewing Kit." See page 138 for more details.

Also, look for stain-resistant overcoats. This will not only help the moisture fall away from the coat during a storm, but will also keep the coat cleaner. Because the overcoat is one item that will last well past the mission if properly cared for, it should be of classic style so it will be useful after the missionary returns home.

Look for a loop to hold a scarf to the overcoat at inside of the neck. Other designs with epaulets on the shoulders make it possible to secure the scarf conveniently under these epaulets.

Overcoats should be purchased in dark, conservative fabrics and styles, usually navy, dark grey, or black. These items are often "dry clean only."

Look for a heavy-duty cloth strap or metal chain at the neckline for hanging the overcoat over a hook. This will make using the coat more convenient and helps it dry on snowy and wet days as it hangs during a discussion or at the missionary's abode!

As with all purchases, this clothing is meant to draw the eye to the face of the missionary so one can listen to the message of the Gospel!

As a Sister explains about cold weather clothing: "You want to buy a bigger coat size in order to fit your shirt and sweater layers underneath. You just layer up as much as you can before you leave the apartment. Some Sisters couldn't fit all their layers under their coats.

"My companion and I weighed ourselves one time with everything on; we weighed 20 pounds more than we usually do. It was hilarious; we were walking marshmallows.

"But you were grateful, because you were outside all day long. And it was nice because when you went inside you could strip off your layers and still be comfortable."

❏ Outerwear, Raincoat.

In warmer, wet areas, a heavier raincoat is less useful than a lightweight one for most seasons of the year. Having a removable lining gives layering options when a cold snap hits. This lining is sometimes designed to be used as a separate, lightweight jacket around the missionary abode.

Some raincoats have a hood that gives additional shelter in wind and heavy weather. If cinching is available at the coat bottom and wrists, even more protection is offered. Styling should be "business conservative."

The fabric of a lightweight raincoat is also very important. It should be water repellant, but don't buy an oversized plastic bag, as the missionary will sweat inside even as he or she is getting wet outside. Some lightweight raincoats are 100% nylon, have air holes to reduce "sweating," and fit into a storage pouch. Always seek for ways to be comfortable in various climates even while finding protection from the rain.

Although we bought raincoats for them, two of our sons that went to countries with hotter climates found it easier to get wet in a rainstorm and dry out naturally than to carry a raincoat. Our two other missionaries were glad for and used their raincoats regularly during the wetter seasons of the year.

Raincoats that can be washed have a long-term advantage over items that are dry clean only. Raincoats should be of plain fabric and darker in color.

Look for a raincoat that zips up the front and also has an overflap that can be snapped in place to protect the zipper. In rough weather, rain easily penetrates exposed zippers. Overflaps to cover pocket openings will also keep the rain out, especially if the pocket openings are slanted. A full-length raincoat that comes almost to the knees, will give more protection when a three-quarters length coat which often comes just to the mid-thigh.

Have the missionary try on the raincoat in the store and wear it around for a while. He or she should be comfortable with no "I am inside a plastic bag feeling." If allowed, put a small amount of clean water in an indention of the coat fabric to see if it really holds the water.

We purchased a nice looking, inexpensive raincoat for one of our sons, only to have him find (after he was in a faraway country) that the fabric saturated with water within minutes of a good rain shower and thus became worse than useless.

A Sister missionary suggests: "I would recommend buying raincoats, overcoats, jackets, anything like that, in the field because you may think you are investing your money wisely and then later find you don't use what you have bought and there are better options for you in the field that experienced missionaries have tried and tested."

❏ Pajamas.

Choose pajamas that are comfortable, medium-weight, and durable. Darker, patterned colors are best, as they will wear longer without showing stains and dirt. Long sleeves and full-length pants out of thicker fabrics are best for colder seasons. They should be overly large so thermals can be worn underneath. Short or mid-length sleeves and calf-length bottoms are better for warmer seasons in cotton or cotton-blend fabrics.

❏ Scarf (for outerwear).

For colder climates, choose a scarf that compliments the overcoat color. It is better if it is about eight to twelve inches wide and 48" to 60" long so it can be worn around the neck and down the front of the body under the coat. This will allow for extra warmth at the neck and chest. At other times, it can be wrapped around the neck and up over the head to protect the face from winter winds, making length and width doubly important.

Consider buying a scarf in a non-scratchy wool, often called "lamb's wool," that is double-layered to add substance and warmth. Acrylic scarves are attractive, but have none of the additional "warming" merits of a woolen scarf. Traditional designs include plaids, stripes, and solid-color scarves.

❑ Shared Clothing.

Every Elder and Sister will have different experiences, but sometimes the missionary will find others have been generous by leaving behind clothing from their wardrobe when they left the mission field. He or she might take advantage of these clothing items when someone else has been generous to them. Then, when they return home, they can consider leaving behind their own, unneeded clothes to bless the lives of future missionaries serving in their area.

A Sister explains: "This is something most Sisters don't know.... usually when you go home you leave some of your old clothing behind in the apartment. So a lot of Sisters would wear the used clothing that was left behind. It was usually still good and was fun to have something else to add to your wardrobe.

"Believe me, I was warmer because I wore some of the big, warm sweaters I got from other Sisters."

❑ Shoes, Tennis.

Tennis shoes should be comfortable, sturdy and can even be a pair the missionary already owns, if they are in good condition. They will often be used as part of the daily exercise program and on Preparation Days for sports, in addition to any work projects the missionary may become involved with during service opportunities.

❏ Shoes, Walking.

See "Specifically For Elders" on page 73 and "Specifically for Sisters" on page 96.

❏ Thermals.

A pair of thermals is helpful for most winter situations and will give the missionary layering options. These will be used night and day in really cold areas and should be "roomy" when purchased and laundered several times before the missionary leaves because they often shrink somewhat.

❏ Work Clothing.

See entries for "Preparation Day Clothing" under "Specifically For Elders" on page 70 and "Specifically for Sisters" on page 95.

Items to Buy and Take – Clothing for Elders and Sisters Checklist

- ☐ Belts.
- ☐ Earmuffs.
- ☐ Flip-flops.
- ☐ Garments.
- ☐ Gloves.
- ☐ Gym clothes. See entries under "Clothing Specifically for Elders" on page 69 and "Clothing Specifically for Sisters" on page 91.
- ☐ Handkerchiefs.
- ☐ Outerwear, Overcoat.
- ☐ Outerwear, Raincoat.
- ☐ Pajamas.
- ☐ Scarf.
- ☐ Shoes, Tennis.
- ☐ Shoes, Walking. See entries under "Clothing Specifically for Elders" on page 73 and "Clothing Specifically for Sisters" on page 96.
- ☐ Thermals.
- ☐ Work Clothing. See entries for "Preparation Day Clothing" under "Clothing Specifically for Elders" on page 70 and "Clothing Specifically for Sisters" on page 95.
- ☐ See "Items to Buy and Take – Clothing Specifically for Elders" on page 65 for additional clothing items for Elders.
- ☐ See "Items to Buy and Take – Clothing Specifically for Sisters" on page 84 for additional clothing items for Sisters.

Items to Buy and Take – Clothing Specifically For Elders

> *"A missionary is expected to dress in a certain way, projecting a clean-cut appearance that includes an appropriate haircut, being clean shaven, wearing a clean white shirt, a tie, and a well-press suit – all the way down to a good shoe shine."* Elder L. Tom Perry, November 2007 *Ensign*, page 48

Some clothing items are particularly for the use of Elders and so this section is written directly to them. These items are listed separately here (in alphabetical order) for the ease of Elders preparing for their missions.

❑ Baptism Clothing, Pants.

It is likely you will baptize while in the field (actually that is the whole point of going) and will need the appropriate baptismal clothing to fill this need.

Choose white pants that are comfortable, flexible at the waist (who knows if you will gain or lose weight during your missionary service) and long enough to almost reach the floor when you are standing in socks. It is easier if this pair of pants is constructed so it doesn't need a belt. They are usually purchased unhemmed.

Wash and dry these pants before hemming to allow for some shrinkage. Many times the fabric of these pants is a polyester blend that means more durability and fewer wrinkles.

Scrunching up the fabric in your hand and then releasing it will tell you a great deal about the quality of the fabric. In some missions, baptism clothing is also available at the chapels.

❑ Baptism Clothing, Shirt.

You will not need to purchase a separate white shirt for this need. One of the long-sleeved white shirts in your missionary wardrobe will do just fine.

❑ Baptism Clothing, Tie.

The tie used for baptisms should be white and washable so it can be dried after each baptism and washed, rinsed, and dried as needed to keep it clean and white.

❑ Boots – Colder Climate Missions.

Choosing the right boots for your mission can be intimidating, but is a very necessary activity. Shop until you are completely satisfied with sturdy, comfortable, warm boots that will keep your feet dry. They should be constructed so water and/or snow cannot easily enter. Some styles are designed so the tongue of the boot and the two sides are sewn together as one piece to accommodate this need.

The boot should come up to lower or mid-calf and have oversized shoelace holders (if a laced-up boot). This allows for easier removal of the boot.

Having a way to cinch the boot top close around the leg will save snow and moisture from entering at that location. Some high quality boots have an additional cinch at the ankle that keeps in warmth and conforms the boot closer to the foot, which makes for surer footing.

Consider buying boots that are oversized in order to allow for several layers of heavy socks. Those with a thicker tread on the sole of the boot will make for additional grip whenever out-of-doors. And, of course, all boots would best be regularly waterproofed to keep feet warm and dry. See page 116 for additional waterproofing information.

In some missions with extreme weather, it is preferable for boots to be purchased in the locality of the mission field to accommodate getting the best boots for that climate. This, of course, creates a dilemma because cold weather clothing might also be needed at the Missionary Training Center. In addition, upon your arrival in the mission field you might be immediately assigned to an area far from stores and shops that carry the needed cold weather clothing. Each situation will demand its own best decisions.

❏ Dress Slacks.

Dress slacks should be durable because they will need to hold their crease, endure many washings, some ironings, and occasional neglect. Blends of 55% polyester/45% wool or 60% wool/40% polyester are common and comfortable. Anything 100% polyester or a polyester/rayon blend is going to be most *uncomfortable*, especially in warm climates, and should be avoided!

As a side note, the lightweight wool used in pants is often called "tropical" wool. It produces a fine sheen on the surface that is very breathable, especially in warmer climates. Wool is like "temperature control" for the body as it adjusts to varying humidity and climate conditions. It also helps insulate the body in colder climates because of this quality.

Slacks should be purchased in solid, dark colors. Black, navy, dark green, dark brown, medium grey, and charcoal are suitable shades. Buying a variety of your favorite colors gives some interest to your wardrobe.

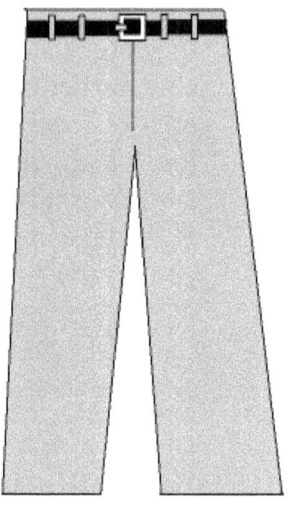

Slacks should fit generously in the waist with a belt used to take up the slack. Usually pants come with a generous two to two and one-half inch rear seam allowance that will allow for further alterations, if necessary.

Slacks often come in a flat front or with double pleats at the waistband. While it is a matter of personal preference, double pleats give pants more fullness and are, therefore, more comfortable for any missionary, especially when sitting and kneeling. This feature is a bit more forgiving for the well-fed missionary, too. It also has the advantage of being cooler because the fabric in this area is farther from the body.

Some slacks come with an ingenious, mostly hidden stretch band on each side at the waist (under a belt loop and just above the seaming of the pocket) that allows for some increase in girth without having to abandon the pants. While every missionary will have a different experience, if you go to a mission

Items to Buy and Take

where you are well fed, it is likely you will gain a bit of weight during these next two years.

If going on a "bike" mission, consider purchasing pants that are lined in the crouch. This lining will help the pants wear longer through many an hour on the bicycle.

Consider doing several knee bends with your pants and a belt on to make sure there is sufficient ease in the crouch of your pants.

Purchase spare spools of heavier thread in the colors of all missionary pants, as this is one clothing item that frequently requires mending, either at the crouch, at the bottoms of the legs, or at the ends of the pockets.

This thread is kept in the Sewing Kit as suggested on page 138. You can also refer to page 189 for specific information on hand mending pants.

While it is a matter of personal choice, pants with cuffs are more stylish but have the disadvantage of filling up with all kinds of "natural" objects during the missionary day such as dust, weeds, dirt, more dust, and an occasional, unwelcome insect.

Therefore, if cuffs are desired, it might be well to put them on suits (which are worn less frequently) and leave them off everyday slacks.

❑ Gym Clothes.

Elders frequently engage in sports on Preparation Day at the Missionary Training Center, in the mission field, and at branch or ward activities. A good pair of modest gym shorts and a sturdy t-shirt will facilitate appropriate dress during these diversions.

These clothes are also often worn around the abode after hours, especially in warmer climates; and therefore, should be modest enough to adequately cover underclothing no matter the sitting, standing or reclining position.

❏ Hat.

Because of the cold, some missionaries may be asked to purchase a hat or woolen cap. Find out exactly what will be acceptable and permissible for your mission before proceeding, as this is a specialty item.

❏ Pants.

See "Dress Slacks" under "Items to Buy and Take – Clothing Specifically for Elders," page 67.

❏ Preparation Day Clothing.

Elders will need appropriate casual clothing for Preparation Day to clean their abode, do laundry, and otherwise prepare for the next week. Shirts should fit comfortably and be in good condition. Pants should be full-length and also in good condition.

❏ Shirts.

Men's shirt sizes usually have two measurements indicating (first) the size of the neck and (second) the length of the sleeve. Shirts should look tailored, fit nicely at several places (shoulders, neck, wrists, and waist) and flow with the shape of the body. A well-fitted, neat and conservative shirt will increase the professional look all missionaries should desire.

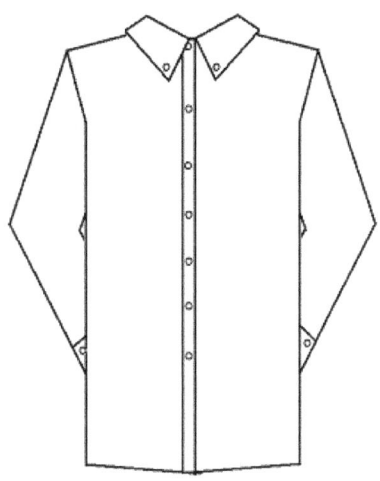

There should be about a one-inch gap from shirt collar to neck when the shirt is buttoned up and pulled forward from the neck with the index finger. Button-down collars are preferred because the collars are always more presentable no matter the state of the shirt, whether wet, wrinkled, dry, or worn. Collars with stays tend to "fly" away from the shirt after many washings.

The full-length shirtsleeve should rest just at the part of the thumb area where it begins to move outward past the wrist. There should be about a ½" to ¾" edge of cuff showing when a shirt is worn with a suit. Wearing cuff links is not preferred because they are usually gold or silver in color, draw undue attention to the missionary, and suggest being wealthy or well-to-do.

Shirts come in two basic fabrics: Broadcloth and Oxford cloth. Each has its advantages and disadvantages. Broadcloth is often a 65% polyester/ 35% cotton fabric, with a smaller thread and tighter weave and therefore is a thinner fabric. This fabric has a smooth sheen to it, is a bit more uncomfortable because of the higher percentage of polyester, but irons up easily, even though it is less durable when hand washed.

Oxford is usually a 60% cotton/40% polyester fabric with a larger thread and more open weave. This fabric has a textured look to it, is very breathable because of the weave and higher cotton content, and is more likely to wrinkle, but is also much more comfortable in both colder and warmer climates. It is a great fabric because it endures hand washing and much abuse in washing machines or at the mercy of a Laundromat, and does reasonably well without ironing. It also has the advantage of making the underclothing less visible.

Always scrunch up shirt fabric in your hand to see how much it wrinkles. Then release the fabric to see how it "reshapes" itself. Less wrinkling means easier maintenance and usually a higher-quality shirt.

A European missionary was jealous because the "broadcloth" missionaries could whip through ironing their shirt every morning with ease while his oxford cloth shirt seemed to resist the iron's magic. It might have been the temperature of the iron or it might have been his skill level, but he didn't feel like his shirt ironing matched that of his peers. However, his shirts seemed to last longer and he was more comfortable on both colder and warmer days. There always seems to be trade offs as you choose your personal preferences.

If there is time before you leave, consider purchasing several different kinds of shirts and trying them out through a couple of wearings, washings, and dryings. After determining what you like best, purchase the remaining needed shirts.

Professional clothiers indicate a missionary wears a shirt an average of 73 times during the two-year missionary period. The shirts need to be of especially high quality, durable fabric, and good construction to endure such "abuse."

Look for shirts on sale in addition to asking for a "clergyman's discount," which will usually save a small amount. It is useful to have a copy of the missionary's call letter to prove his or her upcoming status. Visit outlet malls and ask for a "volume" price cut wherever you shop.

Once I found shirts our missionaries liked and because I knew their neck and sleeve sizes, I "phone shopped" for the shirts first, as there seemed to be a wide spectrum of prices. I worked with various department store managers until I found one that would give me both a volume discount plus the clergy discount.

❏ Shoes, Tennis.

See "Shoes, Tennis" under "Clothing for Elders and Sisters" on page 62.

❏ Shoes, Walking.

In many ways, shoes are the most critical purchase an Elder makes because comfort from the beginning day in the field is at stake. Shopping for this item first and shopping until you find answers that work for you will facilitate a comfortable mission, start to finish. Remember, your feet are one of your most important missionary tools.

Take more shoes than you will think you will need when going to a foreign mission. Sometimes they are hard to find in good quality and often more difficult to receive safely by mail. If you have been "hard" on shoes during your teenage years, it is likely the same pattern will be followed during your mission, so plan and purchase accordingly.

Shoes should be sturdy, well fitting, and have a strong, thick sole. Always be looking for those with a good arch as this lessens foot fatigue. Stitching around the edge of the sole helps the shoes last better. Missionaries often walk in water, glues tend to disintegrate, and shoes otherwise fall apart without this stitching.

Styles with wider, longer "toe boxes" (this is the area near the front of the shoe) are less confining for toes, sit more naturally on the foot, and therefore help avoid ingrown toenails, a common malady of missionaries. You will also be able to walk more naturally.

Shoes are also "nicer" if they are a bit "worn in" before the missionary departs for the Missionary Training Center. This is one of the first purchases we made as it took some time to find just the right kind at the right price and we also wanted time and opportunity for "wearing in."

Shoes should be conservative in style and color, usually cordovan, black, or dark brown, that closely match the color of the dress slacks. Buying shoes in different styles and colors facilitates rotating them because it is easy to know which pair is which.

Remember, shoes are going to wear out, no matter the quality of the brand or cost of the shoe, as there is no such thing as an indestructible shoe. However, several things will extend the life of shoes. Shoes should be rotated daily, giving every pair of shoes at least a 24-hour period of rest, airing, and drying. If there is an insole in the shoe, it should be removed prior to the "airing" to facilitate more of the shoe getting a proper drying. A professional clothier indicates that almost 50% of a shoe's durability comes from this "resting" period between each wearing.

❏ Socks.

Elders will need both everyday dress socks and Preparation Day/work socks.

Buy *roomy*, lightweight, mid-calf or slightly shorter socks for warmer seasons and heavier weight, high-calf socks for colder seasons.

Consider buying at the high end on this item, looking for a good quality wool blend, often called "Windsor" wool by the clothing industry. This kind of sock is cooler in the summer and warmer in the winter. It wicks moisture away from the foot to keep the foot dry no matter the temperature. Cotton blends are also cool in warm temperatures, but because they don't wick as easily, feet tend to feel clammy, wet, and uncomfortable. In addition, wool blend socks last well whether hand or machine-washed. Dark, solid colors that match the color of pants are best!

For convenience, choose one color and style of dress sock for the whole mission to make wash day easier, the matching up of clean socks effortless, and making a new pair of socks from the leftovers of two previous pairs possible. Also, take more than you think you'll need so you won't have to worry about this item for the two years you will be gone.

White socks, usually two to four pairs, will be used on Preparation Day, when playing sports, and at baptisms. All white socks should match in style for convenience on washday.

During your mission field experience, changing into a second pair of fresh socks half way through the day helps the feet stay healthier. This is possible only if missionaries come home for lunch.

Wearing two pairs of socks (both thin when worn during warm weather, one thin and one thick during cold weather) at the beginning of your mission (while your feet are getting strong and callused) saves many of the foot problems missionaries are prone to suffer.

When trying on socks, sit down in a pair of your missionary slacks with one leg crossed over the other knee to make sure that the sock and end of the pant leg overlap slightly even in this position. While there is nothing wrong with bare skin, you will feel more professional if you are "covered."

❑ Sports Protection or Supportive Undergarments.

Buy what fits, works, and will last for 24 months.

❑ Suits.

<u>The Number of Suits to Purchase.</u> In some missions, you will probably use only one suit regularly, and that only on Sundays, at mission conferences, and when traveling. If you take a second suit, it will likely sit in your suitcase for most your mission. In other missions, full suits are required clothing more

often. If going to a colder mission, you will probably use two suits more frequently, one lightweight suit for the nicer days and the second heavier weight suit for the colder, more miserable days.

All my boys' mission clothing lists called for two suits. So we bought two new ones for each of our first three missionaries. Each one of them brought home a nearly new suit which had sat in their suitcase almost the entire time of their service and a fairly used pair of suit pants that matched their nicely used suit coat. Finally, with our last missionary, we sent two suits, one previously used by an older brother and one new. He wore the used suit out and came home with the new suit almost unused. In deciding how many suits to buy (and rather to send both new and/or slightly used suits), consider the instructions given in the Missionary Packet, your own finances and your missionary's history of clothing use. We are glad we sent what was asked, because I feel we were blessed for it with a nearly new suit coming home with each missionary.

The Kind of Suits to Buy. Dark, conservative-colored two-pant suits are better because pants often wear out faster than the coat and two-pant suits are often near the same price as a one-pant suit. It has been wisely suggested by a clothing professional that suits be taken on the mission with both pairs of pants and the pants worn every other time with the suit jacket and that all three pieces are dry cleaned together. This will ensure that aging and fading happen evenly across all three pieces. It will also allow for the pants to air out and freshen completely between wearings.

Buy suits with a sturdy, tighter weave in a durable blend of synthetic and natural fibers. Wool is preferable because of its "climate control" attributes and its resilience. A bit of pattern hides dirt longer.

Some pants are reinforced in the crouch with an addition of an iron-on piece of fabric moving outward from the crotch seam about 3-6." This keeps the pants from wearing quite so quickly. Double seaming in the crouch will also help this area take more wear and tear before splitting open. It is one place where there should be sufficient fullness.

Some suits will come with an interior zippered pocket in the jacket. This is often called a security pocket and is useful for securing the passport, visa, and other documents while traveling.

Some suits come with stain-resistant fabrics or have been stain protected. This is a definite advantage for the occasional, accidental spill and any missionary will be glad for quick and easy cleanups without the hassle of dry cleaning his suit.

Some clothing stores have lifetime alternations. This is financially useful if the missionary matures physically during his mission and needs suit pants or jackets altered upon his return.

<u>The Kind of Suit Style to Consider.</u> Suit styles often include those with two or three buttons. While there may be a preference on the part of each missionary, choose a style that is complimentary to his unique build and personality. Remember, the bottom button on all suit coats is usually left undone.

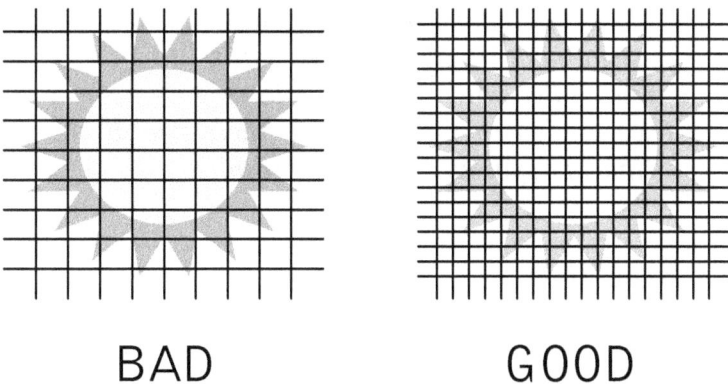

BAD   GOOD

How can you tell the quality and sturdiness of fabric? Hold the fabric on the diagonal between your two hands, which are placed about six inches apart. Stretch the fabric on this bias. If it stretches excessively this is usually a bad sign. If it does stretch but returns to its original shape easily when you let go, this is a good sign. If it doesn't return to its original shape upon releasing, this is another bad sign.

Lift the fabric up onto the light. If the weave is loose and lots of light comes through it is likely a lower quality fabric. However, if the weave is tight and not much light penetrates, this indicates a higher quality fabric.

<u>Getting The Best Fit in a Suit</u>. Don't buy too big of a suit unless you are still growing. Mostly check how the suit lays on the shoulders and how the pants fit

at the waist. Remember that some missionaries lose weight and some gain. Ask other returned missionaries from your mission what is the norm and buy accordingly.

Because our first missionary grew slightly on his mission, we bought "big" for our subsequent missionary who spent his whole mission "swimming" in an oversized suit that he never truly filled into. With our later missionaries we tended to buy closer to their size at the time of departure with good results!

❑ Sweater.

Even in a warmer mission, a lightweight wool-blend V-neck sweater (in a darker, solid color) allows for layering on the chillier days. (In some countries, buildings don't have heat facilities for colder days.)

A V-neck sweater is requested because it shows more of the shirt and tie, whereas the crew cut sweater barely shows the shirt collar and can be misleading. Sweaters are not usually to be worn without a suit coat.

Of course, if going to a colder mission, look for a comfortable, heavier-weight wool sweater with a tighter weave (for greater warmth) to layer as needed. These sweaters often come in charcoal, brown, black, and navy colors.

Occasionally you will find a 70-80% acrylic/20-30% wool blend, machine washable sweater. This has the advantage of being machine or hand washable in cold water and tumble dried, but lessens the advantage of warmth because of the lower wool content.

❑ Ties.

Easy-to-maintain, conservative-patterned ties are best. They should not contain pictures or caricatures, nor be of unusual width or length. All ties should compliment pant and suit colors for easier wardrobe management. They should all look business professional in style, pattern, and color!

Zippered ties work well initially and are convenient, but eventually the zippers seem to give way unless they are maintained with the greatest of care.

Washable ties sound opportune, but often the internal facings are warped by hand washing even through the outer fabric does well, so it is a matter of do you or do you not want to end up with a "limp dishrag" tie? Usually, using a damp cloth or sponge for cleaning is a safer idea.

Not having the facilities to dry clean his ties, one of our sons successfully hand washed several of his ties in warm water and a bit of liquid soap that he then rinsed well and laid flat to dry. Others bled badly and had to be discarded, so proceed with caution!

Non-washable ties often come in polyester or silk fabrics. Most people can't tell the difference, so choose those that are most appealing in design, feel, and price.

The printed colors of silk ties have the disadvantage of bleeding onto shirts in especially hot and humid climates and therefore are not recommended for missions in those areas.

Organize for a Mission

Remember, even as you make the best decisions you know how with the instructions and information which will come with the Missionary Packet, be prepared for occasional correction and additional instruction about clothing standards when you arrive at the Missionary Training Center.

Items to Buy and Take – Clothing Specifically For Elders Checklist

- ☐ Baptism Clothing, Pants.
- ☐ Baptism Clothing, Shirt.
- ☐ Baptism Clothing, Tie.
- ☐ Boots – Colder Climate Missions.
- ☐ Dress Slacks.
- ☐ Gym Clothes.
- ☐ Hat.
- ☐ Preparation Day Clothing.
- ☐ Shirts.
- ☐ Shoes, Tennis. See "Items to Buy and Take – Clothing for Elders and Sisters" on page 62.
- ☐ Shoes, Walking.
- ☐ Socks.
- ☐ Sports Protection or Supportive Undergarments.
- ☐ Suits.
- ☐ Sweater.
- ☐ Ties.
- ☐ See "Items to Buy and Take – Clothing for Elders and Sisters" on page 52 for additional clothing items for Elders.

Items to Buy and Take – Clothing Specifically For Sisters

"Lay aside the things of this world, and seek for the things of a better." D&C 25:10

While serving a mission will leave little time to focus on yourself, it is important your wardrobe be of good quality, good fit, and with a sufficient number of modest clothes. Therefore, this section is written to the Sisters.

As much as possible, coordinate all your new clothing purchases with any previous acquisitions. This will maximize your wardrobe. In other words, have all the blouses go with all the skirts, vests, and jackets. Have all the skirts go with all the blouses, vests, and jackets. Have all the shoes go with all the outfits, and as much as possible, all the accessories interchangeable with all the clothes.

Striving for a professional look, solid colors in sturdy fabrics increase the mixing and matching possibilities. It may seem like clustering in this way will be "tiresome," but in fact it liberates you to have the most variety possible especially with the addition of simple jewelry pieces and several printed scarves.

Polyester fabric wears very well, doesn't wrinkle as much during use and after being washed, but has the disadvantage of not being as comfortable in a wide range of temperatures. In the cold, it is "brittle" cold and in the heat it is "sweaty" hot. Therefore, it is best saved for "best dress" instead of everyday use.

On the other hand, polyester/cotton or polyester/wool blends are the best of both worlds in durable fabrics that don't wrinkle as much and are comfortable in a wider variety of temperatures. The higher the polyester content, the less wrinkling you will have. The higher the natural fiber content, the more comfort you will experience. There always seems to be tradeoffs!

Shopping for Sisters' clothing generally takes longer than for Elders. The styles needed for classic, conservative dress will usually require extensive searching, extra visits to different stores, and an extended period of time. Plan for a substantial amount of time and energy in this direction and then be surprised if it turns out to be easier than planned.

As before, the clothing needs for Sisters are listed here alphabetically for ease in locating specific information.

❑ Blazers.

See "Jackets" under "Items to Buy and Take – Clothing Specifically For Sisters" on page 91.

❑ Blouses.

In this guide, the term "blouse" will be used to distinguish between a men's shirt and a women's. Blouses in solid, light colors are preferable with collars or round necklines. Look for styles that move the eye up to your face. Features that denote femininity will add a note of personality to this piece of clothing.

Make sure blouses have ample room across the shoulders and under the arms. One way you know if a blouse fits well in the body is if you can hunch your shoulders forward and still have ample room across the back of the yoke. A second way is to look at the buttons near the bust line. If there is tension or openings in this area, you may want to consider a larger blouse or a different style. Also, the bottom hem should be finished in a classic style or the blouse should be worn tucked in.

Short sleeves should be about midway down the upper arm to be modest, look professional, and appear flattering. Sleeves half way between the elbow and wrist are very useful for year-round wearing as they can easily be rolled up for warmer weather and yet provide some warmth on the lower arm in cooler temperatures. And, of course, long sleeves are wonderful for the days with chillier temperatures.

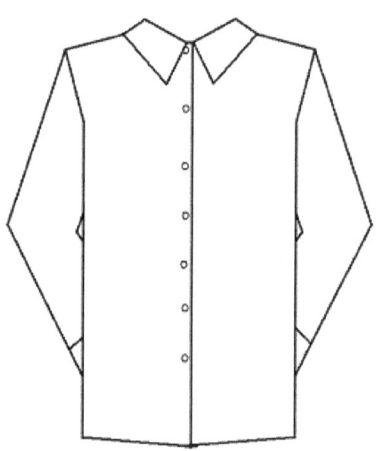

Cotton/polyester or wool/polyester blends give the best combination of breathable, comfortable fabric and easy-to-maintain clothing items. Remember, the higher the polyester content, the less wrinkles you will deal with but the less comfortable the blouse will be in extreme weather.

Scrunch up the blouse fabric in your hand and release it. Does the fabric spring back without a lot of wrinkles? If so, it will do well through innumerable wearings and washings.

Stretch your arms out in front of you to confirm that buttoned, long sleeves have sufficient length for comfort without binding at the wrists. When you return your arms to your sides, make sure the sleeves fall back into place easily.

Because modesty is very important during your mission, look for possible problems. For instance, lean over in front of a mirror to see what happens to the blouse front when it falls downward. Are you still in a modest situation?

Stretch your arms high above your head and then let them drop down again to your sides. Does the blouse fall naturally back to its rightful place around your hips? If so, it is a blouse that will serve you well with the many movements you will make each day without having to tug at the hem to get it back into place again.

Check the buttons on the blouse front and at the wrists for secure sewing. Check the hemming and seaming at the bottom of the blouse. Has the blouse been well sewn and lays flat at all the seams?

A Sister missionary who served in Europe shares her point of view: "Get really nice blouses you like a lot. You might pay more money for them, but you will be wearing them over and over again. Quality blouses last a lot longer and don't look as worn in the end. I recommend nice, button-down blouses that don't pucker anywhere. They have some great fabrics now that don't wrinkle; those are the best kind. You don't want to waste your time ironing.

"Here is what happens: You get home after a long day of tracting and you want to just do your final planning and then head straight to bed. No one ever wanted to stay up taking care of his or her clothes. You are just too pooped (or should be).

"I liked the polyester-blend blouses you could pull out of the dryer and not have to iron. Getting clothes that can be hand or machine-washed is really a must. It is too expensive to get your clothes dry-cleaned all the time, and it is just less of a headache to do so.

"In my mission, the apartments had washing machines, but no dryers. So everyone had dry-racks where they would hang their stuff to dry. No one in other European countries I have since visited had dryers because the electricity over there is too expensive. So get used to having stiff clothes; they don't smell as sweet and aren't as soft as when coming from a dryer!"

A Sister who served in South America had a different experience: "Take into account the economy of the field you are going to. In my mission I did not want to wear really nice clothes. I had brought some, but it felt uncomfortable for me if I wore nice fabrics in a house where someone had a dirt floor and didn't know what they were having for dinner. This is one reason style went out the window. I wanted to feel like the people in my mission and be like them. I wanted them to feel comfortable around me so I had a few jumpers made for me there and it worked out for me. However, if I had gone to a different mission in *the States or a visitors' center, I would have wanted to wear my best."*

❑ Boots – Colder Climate Missions.

Choosing the right boots will take some time and trouble on your part, but shop until you are completely satisfied with a sturdy, low-heeled, comfortable, and warm boots.

As a Sister who went to a colder climate explains: "I would recommend buying your boots one size bigger than you usually wear because you will be wearing up to three pairs of wool socks. Don't buy boots that have higher heels or require too much polishing. Get boots that are really comfortable and easy to walk in. You MUST buy waterproof boots!

"Some poor Sisters would get cute suede boots, only to cry when it started snowing and their toes got all wet. Also, you want your boots to be higher than the hemline of your skirts; otherwise the hemline will get stuck on the zippers of the boots. It is nice if you can shine them once and a while, but not too often.

"I recommend getting boots that zip up rather than those which than have laces. You will be walking into homes for appointments and it is just faster to take them off quickly rather than have to lace them up all the time. I also recommend getting them in black."

❑ Dresses.

Choose dresses that are classic in style, usually solid in color (or with a small print) that will blend easily

Organize for a Mission

with your chosen vests, sweaters, and jackets. Dresses should be from just below the bottom of the knee to mid-calf and cover the knees when sitting. Any piece of clothing, including dresses, increases in value if it has pockets.

When trying on dresses, reach up, forward, and outward with your arms. Then return to a standing position with arms to your sides. How does the dress react when given a chance to return to its normal position? The best dresses don't have to be "put" back into place, they naturally fall back into place. Sit down. Are you also comfortable in this position?

Lean forward and look in the mirror. Are you safely modest wearing the dress even in this situation?

Always purchase dresses of high quality fabric. As with blouses, scrunch up the fabric in your hand and release it. Does the fabric spring back without a lot of wrinkles? If so, it will do well as you work and serve.

Check all seams, pocket linings, zippers, and buttons for secure sewing and ease of use.

❏ Feminine Hygiene Needs.

Discreetly inquire what will be available where you will serve and pack or plan to purchase accordingly.

❏ Gym Clothes.

Because exercise is an important of missionary service and endurance, appropriate, modest gym clothes should be acquired for Preparation Day and sports activities.

❏ Hats.

Different missions have different rules about hats, but if allowed, a warm hat can make each and every day during winter a nicer experience, so spend at the high end on this item, as it is very important for comfort. Remember, because it is taken off frequently, labeling your hat is of special importance so it can be returned if lost!

As a Sister missionary explains: "In some missions you are not allowed to wear certain kinds of hats, but wearing a hat is really important. It is just so cold being outside all day long; you are going to want to cover your head with something."

❏ Jackets.

Jackets (which are sometimes referred to as blazers) should fit well across the shoulders, fall nicely over the hips, be professional in design, be just slightly oversized, and somewhat longer to allow for a sweater and/or vest underneath on the colder days. Depending on the mission, you will wear one every day or just on special occasions.

As mentioned before, scrunch up the jacket fabric in your hand and release it. Does the fabric spring back without a lot of wrinkles? If so, it will do well through innumerable days of use.
Tug on the jacket buttons to check quality of sewing.

Check the hemming and pocket seams for secure seaming. There is nothing more inconvenient than mending when you first arrive in the mission field because you bought poorly made clothes.

A lined jacket is usually better made, will last longer, and will be nicer to wear because it will slip off and on with ease.

Take the jacket on and off several times to check for well-sewn seams, a secure lining, and ease of use.

A Sister explains: "You will have to find out specific dress codes for your mission before you go. Every mission president has different rules. We were required to wear suit jackets only to Zone Conference. Other missions had to wear them every day, so those missionaries had several, while I only had two."

❏ Jewelry.

Small, classic jewelry adds a nice touch to any outfit. For missionary work, it should be simple, small, and not draw attention to itself. Jewelry is meant to compliment, not complicate a Sister's wardrobe.
A Sister missionary shares: "Bring simple jewelry to spice up your outfits."

Another Sister adds: "I wore the same pair of earrings throughout my mission. If you have pierced ears, you may want to consider this. If not, small simple jewelry is the best so as to not detract from the Spirit of your call and the reason you are there. I also had a very simple necklace I wore. While it is personal preference, simple and non-distracting is the most important thing here."

❏ Jumpers.

Jumpers in darker, neutral colors like navy, charcoal, black, dark brown or dark green serve a Sister well. Some convenient styles have two buttons on each of the shoulders.

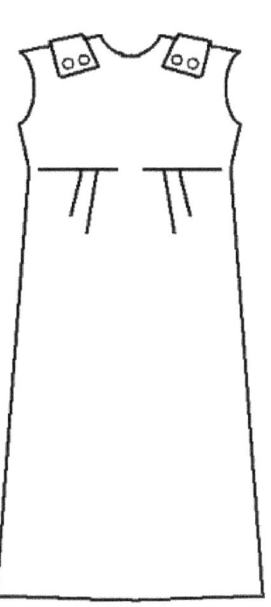

Jumpers should be made of sturdy fabric, be resilient in style, and sit on your body amply around the bust line and hips. When you lift your arms and then let them fall again, the jumper should return to its original place naturally. Fabric should be a blend that doesn't wrinkle easily, won't need ironing after washing, and even looks great after being hung to dry. Pockets are a plus! Any clothing items made of denim, leather, or "wrinkly" fabrics are not appropriate.

Because jumpers are to be from just below the knee to mid-calf and cover the knees when sitting, it may take some extra shopping and maybe even the purchase of a floor-length item that is then altered to the right length.

As always, scrunch up the jumper fabric in your hand and release it. Does the fabric spring back without a lot of wrinkles? If so, it will amply meet your needs. If not, you may want to continue shopping until you find more suitable fabrics.

Check the jumper zipper for ease of use and durability by opening and closing it several times. Check the hem and pocket seaming. Has the jumper been well sewn? Also, check pocket linings for sufficient depth, sturdy fabric, and secure seams.

A Sister who served in South America advises: "Cotton fabrics were the best for my mission since it breathed the best in the heat. I thought linen dresses or skirts were comfortable and light, but they were always wrinkly and did not represent our call well, as we didn't iron much in my mission.

"The most comfortable (but not always most stylish) articles that we wore were the jumpers. Style went out the window for me in the mission and I resorted to COMFORT as the most important. Loose jumpers were the best because of my hot mission."

❑ Leggings - Colder Climate Missions.

Leggings are an option to consider, even if they are shorter than your skirts or jumpers, because they will keep the upper part of your legs warmer.

As a Sister who served in a colder climate explains: "I wish I had brought along a pair of warm leggings. It would have been a lot warmer to wear them under a skirt. You could wear leggings and then wear tights over them and no one would ever know under your boots."

❑ Nylons.

Nylons are no longer required at the Missionary Training Center. However, if you desire to wear them, choose nylons that are comfortable, sturdy, and will hand wash easily.

Try wearing several different kinds for a couple of weeks before you make your final purchases, as some nylons are uncomfortable at the waist, others bind in the crouch, and some just don't last very long. It is preferable to get nylons with reinforced toes, as they tend to be more durable.

Of course, with some clothing you can wear knee high hose if the top of this hose doesn't show under any circumstances.

❑ Preparation Day Clothing.

Choose heavy-duty, durable tops and pants that are loose fitting and will be modest on your body wet or dry. You don't want your clothing to be too revealing should you get caught in the rain or have water splashed on you. Pants should be full-length and comfortably loose.

Be sensitive that your Preparation Day clothing does not have labels, wording, or anything else that would demean your stewardship. Missionaries are missionaries all the time!

❑ Scarves.

Scarves can somewhat inexpensively add variety and interest to your wardrobe.

As a Sister missionary explains: "It was nice to have a variety of scarves (different colors and sizes) because your outfits just got boring. It spiced things up with a pretty scarf."

❏ Shirts.

See "Blouses" under "Items to Buy and Take – Clothing Specifically For Sisters," page 85.

❏ Shoes, Tennis.

See "Shoes, Tennis" under "Items to Buy and Take – Clothing For Elders and Sisters," page 62.

❏ Shoes, Walking.

Shoes are a very personal purchase. However, function should reign over beauty during a mission. There will be plenty of time later for "higher heeled, fancier" shoes. For now, choose the most comfortable, sturdy shoes you can find. Shoes should be close-toed and closed-heeled. Always search for shoes with a good arch and roomy shoe "toe boxes." Bigger is often better, and yes, the "old lady styles" are sometimes the best. Observe women who stand on their feet all day long and see what they wear. This will give you a clue as to your best purchases.

As a Sister explains: "I think most Sisters think they will just be strolling along. No, you will have a sense of urgency, walking fast and will be very active. Get skirts and boots that you can run for the bus in! Get very comfortable shoes. Don't be afraid to spend a little more money on them; the better quality will last almost your whole mission. I brought four pairs of shoes: Black shoes, brown shoes, black boots, and nicer black shoes for Zone Conferences."

Another Sister who served overseas comments: "I found a pair of shoes I liked that were sturdy and comfortable. My mom had the good idea to buy two pairs of the same shoe. This turned out to be brilliant because the first pair wore out and I already had a replacement pair with me whose style I liked."

A Sister who served in South America advises: "I bought two very nice pairs of shoes. Every single missionary I knew had blisters and bled around their ankles and on their toes for the first few months of their missions, every single one of them. I had a very "walking" mission. We probably walked ten to fourteen miles/day. These missionaries were in severe pain for several months. I did not have one single blister in my entire mission, and I also never bought a replacement pair of shoes. I rotated these shoes, one black and one brown, throughout my mission and was able to pass them on to be used by other missionaries when I left the mission. I have a big testimony in purchasing good quality shoes for a mission!"

❏ Skirts.

Skirts are one of the more important clothing items a Sister buys. Skirts should fit comfortably at the waist (about one inch of space when pulled away from the waist, which will more easily allow blouses to be tucked in). They should sit easily on the hips, move with your body when you walk, and not twist and turn as you move.

Take a short walk around the store before purchasing and wash/dry each one afterwards to make sure the skirt holds its shape and original size.

Just as you may have done with other items, scrunch the skirt fabric up in your hand and then release it. Is the fabric still beautiful, unwrinkled, and stable? This is an important factor because you will be sitting in these skirts for many hours and sometimes days. You want them to be workable in many situations.

A skirt that is lined has the advantage of being nicer to wear as your body will move inside the slippery lining easily and be more comfortable because of the double layering. Skirts usually last longer, too, if they are lined because the lining takes part of the wear and tear.

Check the zipper and button on the skirt for ease of use and durability. Finally, check if the hem and pocket seaming has been well secured. Remember, any slits in skirts or jumpers should not reach above the knee, even when sitting.

If you will be riding a bike, your skirt (or jumper) will need sufficient fullness to allow you to modestly mount your vehicle. The best way to decide if this is possible is to split your legs about 3-4' apart with the skirt or jumper on. Can you do this with ease? If so, you will be able to handle getting on a bike modestly!

As a Sister missionary explains: "I was transferred to a bike area at the end of my mission, and that transformed my wardrobe completely. If you are riding a bike, you need a skirt that will be long enough so when you are pedaling it won't ride up. You will need a skirt that doesn't have slits and is really full at the bottom so that you can get up on a bike with no problem."

❑ Slips.

In general, wearing a slip helps with modesty, lets your clothing move around on your body with ease, and even keeps you warmer on those colder days. Purchase half and/or whole slips that are comfortable, especially at the bust line, waist, and hips, and nearly the length of your hems.

When trying on a slip, move your extended arms back and forth, up and down, bend over several times, and otherwise stretch to see if the slip works with or against you.

If you will be riding a bike, you will need a slit in the slip to allow you to mount the bike comfortably and modestly.

❑ Socks.

Again, socks are very personal choices. However, conservative, sturdy socks will give you flexibility and durability. Look for wool blends and try on all socks for comfort and fit. Preparation Day socks should be durable and easy to maintain, too.

Because each mission has its own needs, purchase with care. For instance, a Sister who served in a hotter country, shares: "In my mission we did not regularly wear nylons, only socks, because of the heat."

❏ Suits.

Suits are a jacket and skirt both made of the same material. A tailored suit has the advantage of looking formal, professional, and coordinated. A Sister would do well to take a suit on her mission that she can wear for "best" occasions and also wear with complimenting pieces such as jumpers, vests, and blouses during weekday activities.

A darker, solid-color suit with a lighter blouse tends to help people take you and your message seriously. As with all other pieces of clothing, look for sturdy seaming, well-made pockets, and high-quality fabrics. Remember the scrunch test? Because suits tend to be more costly, take a longer period of time to check out construction quality, fabric type, and ease of care.

❏ Sunday Clothes.

While it is true you want to look your best every day of your mission, wear something unique and/or different on Sundays and at mission conferences to set those days apart. This will make the Sabbath singular and also designate the conferences as special.

A Sister explains: "Have a special shirt, jacket and/or shoes set aside for nicer events like church. You are also going to want a nicer outfit for Zone Conference. It is just nice to get a little more dressed up. We always looked a little more formal on Sundays because we wanted to look pleasingly dressed for the members."

❏ Sweaters.

Sweaters are an important addition to a Sister's wardrobe, both for warmth and for variety. Choose a classic style in a solid color that will augment and compliment the other clothes that have been purchased or gathered.

A sweater with buttons can be easily removed without messing up your hair or putting your arms above the head (which is usually not convenient in public) and therefore is preferable. It is a suggested clothing item if going to the Missionary Training Center during milder fall or springtime weather.

❏ Tights.

Tights are heavier, longer socks that make for great comfort in colder climate missions. Some tights should be large enough to allow for leggings and/or another pair of tights to be worn underneath on the colder days. Choose colors that allow for easy matching with your wardrobe.

As a Sister who served in Europe explains: "All the Sisters wore black or brown tights depending on the color of their skirts. I found that black was just easier for mixing and matching."

❏ Underclothing.

Choose underclothing that is modest, white or cream in color and of the best construction. This is one purchase where you will want to take your time and spend wisely. All clothes look better over well-constructed, sturdy, and modest underclothing.

❏ Vests.

The addition of several vests will fill out your wardrobe, add variety to your attire, and also give you a more dignified, formal look. Choose vests in solid colors or with small prints, matching some of your skirts to wear together for the more formal occasions and yet offsetting other outfits for weekday missionary work.

Even as you do your best with the instructions and information that will come with the Missionary Packet, occasional correction and additional instruction about clothing standards may be received when you arrive at the Missionary Training Center! As it is followed, your capacity as a missionary will increase, both for your obedience and because of your example to others.

Items to Buy and Take – Clothing Specifically For Sisters Checklist

- ☐ Blouses.
- ☐ Boots – Colder Climate Missions.
- ☐ Dresses.
- ☐ Feminine Hygiene Needs.
- ☐ Gym Clothes.
- ☐ Hats.
- ☐ Jackets.
- ☐ Jewelry.
- ☐ Jumpers.
- ☐ Leggings – Colder Climate Missions.
- ☐ Nylons.
- ☐ Preparation Day Clothing.
- ☐ Scarves.
- ☐ Shoes, Tennis. See "Items to Buy and Take – Clothing for Elders and Sisters" on page 62.
- ☐ Shoes, Walking.
- ☐ Skirts.
- ☐ Slips.
- ☐ Socks.
- ☐ Suits.
- ☐ Sunday Clothes.
- ☐ Sweaters.
- ☐ Tights.
- ☐ Underclothing.
- ☐ Vests.
- ☐ See "Items to Buy and Take – Clothing for Elders and Sisters" on page 52 for additional clothing needs.

Items to Buy and Take – Additional Useful Items

"Organize yourselves; prepare every needful thing..." D&C 88:119

In addition to clothing, larger investments, and items specific to gender, there are other items that will make life easier, more convenient, and otherwise "civilized" while serving a mission. Choose these with care, but don't overspend, as you will want to feel free to share and use these items without concern. As before, this section is written to the missionary.

❑ **Alarm Clock.**

Some missionaries successfully use their wristwatch as a personal alarm clock. Others find it easier to have a separate alarm clock with large, illuminated numbers that can be seen both night and day. It is usually more convenient to have a battery-run alarm clock. Spend more than not on this item as it is at the cheaper end anyway and needs to last a good 18-24 months of wear, tear, moving, and using. Purchase a spare set of alarm clock batteries. Put in the Spares Kit (see page 141).

A Sister who served in South America shares: "I took a small alarm clock with a temperature gauge and date. This was the most fun item I took. I loved knowing what the temperature was in my room and also took this small, almost pocket-sized fold-up alarm clock with me out during the day sometimes, just so I could see the temperature while I was walking. It ended up being a very worthwhile purchase both for its functions and its small size."

❑ Backpack.

While a backpack is not usually used while proselyting, it is useful in many other ways. The backpack should be in good condition. Consider carrying a plastic bag in the bottom of the backpack so when it threatens rain or snow, backpack items can be enclosed and protect from the moisture.

We chose to send a backpack with each of our missionaries. They frequently used it to handle luggage overflow on transfer day. Other times they used it to hold dirty clothes on the way to do their laundry or to bring groceries home from the store. It was just a handy tool to have on hand.

❑ Bed Pillowcases.

Take two or more pillowcases that are new or nearly new. Especially if you suffer from acne, you can rotate clean pillowcases on your pillow until laundry day to keep your face happy.

❑ Bed Sheets.

Usually the Missionary Packet will request two, flat single-bed sheets (also called twin sheets) which are new or nearly new. Darker colors and patterned sheets will last better without looking dirty between washings. You will likely be sleeping in and making a lot of various-sized beds, which is why flat sheets (instead of fitted sheets) are suggested.

❑ Consecrated Oil Container.

A small, consecrated oil container, usually attachable to a key chain, is sufficient for most needs. While they come in several different colors, the containers found in both silver and golden tones look conservative and classic.

If this is filled with oil before leaving on the mission, put the consecrated oil container in double protection so it doesn't spill during travel. Usually, two small, twisted plastic bags, one inside the other, do the job nicely. You won't want to seal the bags because of air pressure changes at different altitudes when flying.

❑ Converters and Adapters/Transformers.

These items can be very confusing at first. There are two needs:

1) Transforming voltage; and, 2) Making personal electrical appliances useful through the use of differently configured plugs. If you will be serving overseas, it is possible you will need both converter plugs and a transformer for your electrical tools.

Read the instructions carefully to discern if you are purchasing the right converters for your mission. Often a kit will indicate that it has a transformer in addition to the converter plugs for various international uses.

Purchase a transformer alone when only the voltage needs to be changed. Sometimes this is not necessary, as the electrical appliances will have a switch that will change or "transform" the voltage from 110V to 220V and vice versa.

In the most complex situations, the individual country's converter plug goes into the wall, a transformer is plugged into that plug, and then the appliance is plugged into the transformer.

❑ Flashlight.

When it is dark, there is nothing quite like a small, durable flashlight to keep a missionary feeling safe and happy.

There are several features to look for when purchasing a flashlight. For instance, flashlights that can be hung from a flip-out handle or a hole in the flashlight can function easier as general room lighting during a blackout. A flashlight that is sturdy enough to endure dropping will last longer. A flashlight that uses standard batteries makes it possible to retrieve batteries from other items to use in an emergency.

Bring an extra bulb and several extra sets of batteries. These are kept in the Spares Kit (see page 141).

❑ Hair Care Appliances (for Sisters).

Sisters will always want to look their very best. If needed, durable hair care appliances plus washing hair frequently will make a great deal of difference in your looks, perspective, and confidence. Take what you need, what you will use, and what will make hair care easier each and every day.

❏ Hangers.

Take enough hangers to get your wardrobe hung up, plus a few extra for wet items. A dozen or so should be enough. Sturdy, plastic hangers are a good choice. It is helpful if they are all one color. Then when things get mixed up or left around in your abode, it will be easy to know which hangers are yours. These items take up a lot of room in suitcases so prepare to pack around and inside them to make best use of your limited space.

Metal hangers tend to rust when used to hold wet laundry and should be avoided for that reason.

❏ Insoles.

If you purchased footwear with insoles, it is wise to keep a backup pair in the Spares Kit (see page 141). While the quality may be sufficient for an eighteen-month to two-year use, losing or wearing out insoles makes the shoes almost useless unless replacements are near at hand.

❏ Laundry Bag.

Because the mission experience inevitably produces dirty laundry, a good-sized laundry bag proves helpful for all missionaries. It should be about 3' x 4' in size, in the shape of a pillowcase, and have double strings to draw it closed at one end. There should also be a loop of fabric to allow it to be hung from a hook. The fabric should be durable, the stitching secure, and the strings thick and strong. If the fabric is breathable (such as a mesh cloth), so much the better, especially in humid climates. If is it a darker fabric with a pattern it will go longer without looking dirty.

Items to Buy and Take

❑ Luggage Locks.

Luggage locks usually can't be used when traveling by air, but can add a measure of security either to protect private papers or keep others from prying into confidential possessions during missionary service. It is better to buy sturdy locks, as they will last better than the ones that frequently come with luggage.

Keep the luggage keys in two different places, possibly one set on your key chain and the second in your backpack or shoulder bag. If one is lost or misplaced, the second set can easily be retrieved and used.

❑ Makeup and Makeup Container (again, for the Sisters).

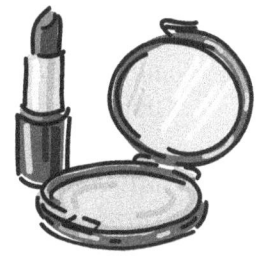

Take simple makeup to enhance but not complicate your features. It is important to look "comely" at all times while in the mission field.

A Sister shares about her European experience: "Bring and wear makeup. You want to look your best as a representative of the Church. I would get frustrated with some of those frumpy Sisters that took no regard for their appearance. People will take you seriously if you are clean and well-groomed."

A Sister who served in South America adds about her hot mission: "I sweat my makeup off within the first hour outside. But makeup was good to have for Zone Conferences and on Sundays.

"Simple is better. Chapstick was also an essential for me.

"I was sorry I brought my big plastic fold-out case of makeup. I could have put a few makeup essentials in a small bag to meet my needs as space in my luggage was so precious!"

❏ Missionary Bag.

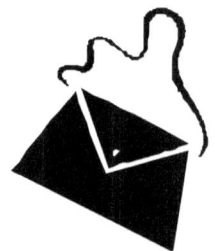

It is best to consider purchasing the missionary bag once on your mission. Missionaries are more likely to get what the mission president permits and a bag similar to what other missionaries are using.

Missionary bags turned out to be a very cultural thing and all our missionaries came home with a different kind of missionary bag, so I am glad we didn't buy this beforehand. So, hold off and let this be a purchase after you have entered the field.

Many a missionary, especially in their early service, has a mission bag too big and heavy to be useful. Learning what you must take, what you should take, and what you might take inside your bag during proselyting means learning to leave most of everything at your abode. Again, remember to carry a plastic bag with you to protect the contents in case of inclement weather.

Items to Buy and Take

A Sister shares: "Don't get a huge bag to carry around. I thought I would be carrying my huge English triple combination around with me, so I got this briefcase-sized bag to carry around. It only broke my back. Get a small, conservative shoulder bag that has pockets. You will carry copies of the Book of Mormon and your planner should be easily accessible to get the phone number and addresses of investigators."

A Sister who served in South America adds: "I would not recommend buying a shoulder bag before you get to the mission field. A lot of missionaries spend good money on a nice bag they don't end up using. Before you go to the field, you may think the bag is small and will not weigh you down much, but 99% of the bags I saw bought before the field were left in apartments in the mission. The reason is because even one more Book of Mormon or something else to carry makes a big difference when you are carrying it for eleven hours a day across town.

"Most of the Elders in my mission found ways to put everything they needed in their many pockets on their pants and shirts (even though they bulged) and carried a Book of Mormon in their hands. The Sisters found small shoulder bags that worked for them, depending on what was needed."

❑ Music CDs.

Music CDs of an appropriate nature are allowed in the mission field. Take as many or as few as will suit your needs, personality, and the need to primarily focus on missionary work.

Take only CDs which are you willing to have used by others, lost, stolen, or ruined during your experience. If you choose this way, such losses won't weigh heavy on you or your relationships with companions and other associates in the field. Always follow the specific music selection guidelines set forth by your mission president and allow considerable time each day for "silence" to feel the promptings of the Spirit.

❑ Pens and Pencils.

Because a missionary does a lot of writing, you should have a good supply of permanent, archival pens that will work well for you. They are used for journal writing and at study time, in addition to when you proselyte. Pencils are convenient for more casual writing needs.

We found it better to purchase and try out several kinds because a pen becomes a very personal matter and one of great consternation if it doesn't work, leaks, smears, or otherwise is troublesome. One of our sons liked roller ball pen; another preferred the "four-colors-in-one" ballpoint pens (as he scheduled his day using the red, green, black and blue pen colors).

❑ Safe, Body.

There are two major kinds of "body safes," one which is worn around the neck and down on the chest and another that is worn at the waist. These hold money and documents while traveling. The chest pouch has the disadvantage of being easily seen under missionary shirts or blouses. The waist pouch can be moved around to the side of the hip and be under the jacket or suit coat, and therefore more secure.

This safe is especially for the Sisters' use and its purchase will depend on what other "secure" places are available in clothing when traveling.

❑ Shoe Bags.

Shoe bags are not common or even convenient to purchase, but prove beneficial to the missionary who doesn't want to get surrounding items dirty when traveling. They are usually made of cloth roomy enough to fit easily over footwear and sometimes come as part of a luggage set.

❑ Spray Bottle.

A good spray bottle will save many a "bad hair" day for both Elders and Sisters. Choose one that is small, durable and has a good spray mechanism.

❑ Sunscreen.

Missionaries have the potential of getting sunburned during their first weeks of tracting. One smaller bottle of sunscreen will help with the transition and to keep them "cooler" in the sunshine during the first month or so until they have an adequate tan. Lip sunscreen will help keep the lips from blistering.

Organize for a Mission

❑ Three-ring Binder, Lined Paper, and Sheet Protectors.

Often, especially in foreign countries, the paper size and binder quality is somewhat different. Packing some "normal" paper and high-quality sheet protectors from home inside a sturdy binder allows time for transition to local sources. It also makes it easy to keep letters from home (or emails that have been printed off), especially if those letters are on standard-sized paper and have been three-hole punched. Mementos can be stored in the sheet protectors, as desired.

❑ Toiletries and Toiletries Bag.

Every missionary will need a good supply of toiletries to begin his or her missionary service. These should be items with which he or she is comfortable. There is no need to be stressed in this area of life when all else will be new and different.

Purchase enough toiletries to last through the Missionary Training Center experience and into the mission field by a month or two. This will allow time for transition and increased knowledge of local sources before worrying about buying "more shampoo."

A toiletries bag with a zipper pull at each end of a wide opening across the top makes it easier to reach in and get items. Another style unzips freely and the opening can then be widened to accomplish the same need.

Items to Buy and Take

Each missionary should consider bringing the following:

- Comb
- Dental floss
- Deodorant
- Hand soap
- Lotion
- Shampoo
- Toothbrush
- Toothpaste

Missionaries may also want to consider:

- Foot powder
- Hair brush
- Hair gel
- Lotion
- Mouthwash

❑ Umbrella.

Take a sturdy, easy-to-open and close umbrella in a neutral color. The small, lightweight ones are convenient to pack around. Try opening and closing it several times before purchasing it and spend more than less on this item. Look for double-pronged umbrellas that are designed to withstand turning inside out in strong winds. Inexpensive, poorly made umbrellas are usually not good enough.

For the most part, our missionary sons didn't use their umbrellas much in warmer climates. The day was too long. If they took their umbrella, it wouldn't rain or would just rain a little and they carried an umbrella around through a lot of sunshine. Or when it rained, it rained sideways and didn't do a bit of good. So usually they just got wet, found a way to get dry again, and kept going with their daily schedule.

On the other hand, our European missionary wouldn't have done without his umbrella. While he left it behind on "light" rain days, it got regularly used during the colder "drench" season.

❑ Washcloths, Hand Towels, and Bath Towels.

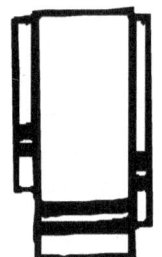

Bring one or two bath towels and one or two hand towels. Bring eight or more washcloths so you will have one for each day of the week and one spare to use while the laundry is being done.

Choose lighter weight towels and washcloths so they will dry more quickly. There is nothing quite as bad as drying off today's shower water with yesterday's wet towel, especially in humid conditions. Darker colors will show dirt less and look nicer when washed by hand! Also, if there is room in the luggage, bring another eight or so washcloths to be used in the kitchen. These are invaluable to keep things tidied up around the apartment and should be of a different color than the washcloths used for personal hygiene.

❑ Waterproofing Gel, Paste, or Spray.

Most shoes and boots survive numerous types of moisture exposure if waterproofed regularly. If you have a choice, buy some good paste waterproofing (instead of gel or spray), as it will, if applied as directed, better help protect footwear from the elements.

❑ Writing Materials.

As you will be writing occasional letters during your stay at the Missionary Training Center, purchase stationery or lined paper that is a standard size (8.5" x 11" is best), can be easily three-hole punched, and promptly kept in a binder. Then when these letters arrive home, your family and friends can enjoy and store them easily. Leave ample margins around the edges of your letters so water damage, potential tearing, and three-hole punching won't ruin or confuse your message.

Both at the Missionary Training Center and once on your mission, much of your communication home may be via email. It will be important that your parents or another trusted individual print, save, and store hard copies of these emails in addition to creating, sorting, and saving computer files of these communications so you have the long-term capacity of preserving your missionary experiences.

❑ Ziploc Bags.

Ziploc bags are useful for securing liquids when traveling or during storage. Take several with you. If ziploc bags are used when traveling by air, do not close the ziploc seal as air pressures change at different altitudes, which present its own issues. Instead, fold one bag around the item and put this bag into a second bag that is folded the other direction, thus reducing the chance that liquids will be released and cause damage.

Items to Buy and Take – Additional Useful Items Checklist

- ☐ Alarm Clock.
- ☐ Backpack.
- ☐ Bed Pillowcases.
- ☐ Bed Sheets.
- ☐ Consecrated Oil Container.
- ☐ Converters and Adapters/Transformers.
- ☐ Flashlight.
- ☐ Hair Care Appliances (for the Sisters).
- ☐ Hangers.
- ☐ Insoles.
- ☐ Laundry Bag.
- ☐ Luggage Locks.
- ☐ Makeup and Makeup Container (again, for the Sisters).
- ☐ Missionary Bag.
- ☐ Music CDs.
- ☐ Pens and Pencils.
- ☐ Safe, Body.
- ☐ Shoe Bags.
- ☐ Spray Bottle.
- ☐ Sunscreen.
- ☐ Three-ring Binder, Lined Paper, and Sheet Protectors.
- ☐ Toiletries and Toiletries Bag.
    Essential:
    - Comb
    - Dental floss
    - Deodorant
    - Hand soap

Items to Buy and Take – Additional Useful Items Checklist
(continued)

- ☐ Toiletries and Toiletries Bag.
    Optional:
    - Foot powder
    - Hair brush
    - Hair gel
    - Lotion
    - Mouthwash

- ☐ Umbrella.
- ☐ Washcloths, Hand Towels, and Bath Towels.
- ☐ Waterproofing Gel, Paste, or Spray.
- ☐ Writing Materials.
- ☐ Ziploc Bags.

Other Financial Needs To Consider

"We urge adherence to the rule of missionary support – namely that it is the responsibility of the individual and the family to provide support for the missionary. This must be encouraged..." Gordon B. Hinckley, *Teachings of Gordon B. Hinckley*, page 349

After purchasing clothing, expensive equipment, and additional items, it is sometimes distressing to think that mission preparation financial needs are just beginning. However, it is usually better to know beforehand than to be surprised. This section is written specifically to parents because there are some additional expenditures that may need your attention.

❑ Cash for the Missionary Training Center.

The Missionary Packet will usually indicate that a certain amount of cash is to be brought to the Missionary Training Center for miscellaneous expenses, additional supplies, and sundries. Get this money in cash and keep it in a safe place until it is time to pack the missionary's luggage.

Missionaries traveling to an overseas Missionary Training Center are also usually asked to have some traveling cash with them. Sending more cash with the missionary than is requested can cause wastefulness, diversionary activities, and otherwise keep the missionary from focusing where he or she should.

❑ Driver's License Renewal Costs.

Missionaries carry a current driver's license or identification card with them as part of their identity needs. This license needs to be "good" until after they return from their mission.

Sometimes your missionary will also drive during the mission, which makes a current driver's license all the more necessary. Contact your local Department of Motor Vehicles to find out how the rules work in your area. Follow their instructions carefully and completely to avoid last-minute problems.

Because we did not understand the implications of this need, my son and I found ourselves standing in the DMV line on the morning of his departure trying to get his driver's license properly extended before he left on his noon flight overseas.

Unhappily, we encountered an official who insisted, despite my son's missionary attire, his missionary tag, and his short, evenly tapered hair that we return home, get our "official mission call" letter, and drive back to the DMV before this particular official would consider that our son was indeed leaving the country and needed a driver's license extension sufficient to accommodate his absence from the country for two years. Oh, such is the learning curve that never quite leaves as each missionary is sent off!

❏ Food and Paper Products.

It is likely that a special gathering of family and friends will take place before your missionary leaves and again when he or she returns. This can get expensive by the time a meal is provided, dessert served, and paper products purchased. Let others contribute, but also wisely budget sufficient funds specifically for these two occasions.

❑ Gas and Other Transportation Costs.

While every missionary's departure will be of a different nature, gas for traveling to the airport, transportation depot, or the Missionary Training Center, plus any meals, lodging, or other travel expenses must be taken into account. There will possibly be additional transportation costs for your family upon your missionary's return. These funds, both for the current needs and for the homecoming needs should be set aside as soon as possible. This helps alleviate surprises and stress along the way. Can you begin to feel the pinch in your wallet again?

❑ Passport Preparation.

This is one of the first preparation activities for the missionary because of the sometimes-lengthy turnaround time, so it is a high priority right after the call is received. A specific kind and size of photo is needed with your missionary in missionary attire.

As we sent out our missionaries, I found the cost of this passport photo varied greatly from place to place. I learned to call around a bit to find who did it for less, produced the finished photos right on the spot, and was knowledgeable about trimming the passport photos to their proper size. This phone shopping saved us considerable time and hassle.

❑ Phone Calls.

Missionaries usually get to talk to their parents and immediate family twice a year, once on Mother's Day and again at Christmas. This expense can be higher if the missionary is overseas. Check well beforehand different avenues for making the phone calls and check twice to make sure the sequencing of numbers you have written down to get to the country, then to the area, then to the city, and then to the location of the phone is CORRECT.

When one of our missionaries was serving, we tried to call on Christmas Day and found that the sequence of numbers we dialed ended up at a dead-end recording. It took us almost an hour, several calls to various different departments of the phone company (and this on Christmas Day) to discover we had erroneously been told to dial one too many ones at the beginning of the call. With this event being so important to both family and missionary, CHECK TWICE to make sure you have correct information before the time and date to call.

It is also important to have a backup time and date to call should the first attempt to connect fail you for some reason.

One of our missionaries initiated the Mother's Day call at his end and wasn't successful in getting through because of busy lines. Then he had to leave the member's home in order to meet mission rules and be in his own apartment by a certain hour. He got permission from his mission president to call again on the next day.

We didn't know why he hadn't called on Mother's Day and we weren't there the next day the first time he tried to call. Subsequently, we arranged both primary and secondary times and dates to make contact with our missionaries.

❑ Postage.

As missionaries communicate through various mail services while at the Missionary Training Center except for writing emails to their immediate family members, receiving regular letters and occasional packages is wonderful. The postage for these mailed letters and packages might best be part of the budget because over the ensuing weeks you will want to be generous in your communication. Especially if your missionary is learning a foreign language, these letters and packages keep up spirits, encourage focused study, and facilitate diligent learning.

❑ Shots and Preventive Medications, Pre-Mission.

Educate yourself about what will be needed, where these services can be obtained, and the timing needed for full protection. These procedures can also be expensive. I found it timely to call my regular doctor's office, the County Health Department, and other possible sources to compare prices and availability. Some shots are occasionally in short supply and are given on a first-come, first-served basis. Other preventive medications are administered in a series of tablets that need to be taken at certain times and under specific conditions to be effective. This is one place where you start early, become informed, and follow directions completely!

Make sure to get written evidence of the immunizations being administered, as your missionary will need this time and time again.

❏ **Shots, Missionary Training Center.**
Some immunizations come in a series and occasionally the latter one is administered in the Missionary Training Center because of time constraints. Your missionary will be responsible to pay for this procedure and will need the funds to do so. It is beneficial to check with your health insurance company to see if the cost of these particular procedures is covered by your insurance.

Other Financial Needs To Consider Checklist

- ❑ Cash for the Missionary Training Center and Traveling.
- ❑ Driver's License Renewal Costs.
- ❑ Food and Paper Products.
- ❑ Gas and Other Transportation Costs.
- ❑ Passport Preparation.
- ❑ Phone Calls.
- ❑ Postage.
- ❑ Shots and Preventive Medications, Pre-Mission.
- ❑ Shots and Preventive Medications, Missionary Training Center.

Preparation of Essential Kits

"Be prepared in all things when I shall send you... to... the mission with which I have commissioned you." D&C 88:80

Preparing several "kits" for the missionary's comfort and keeping will make all the difference, especially during the first weeks and months of the mission experience when all will be somewhat strange, the language somewhat difficult (if he or she is speaking another tongue or even a difficult dialect), and the availability of items possibly in question.

Think carefully about daily routines and what items would be helpful for your missionary's personal needs. Even if items are available at local stores, it is much easier to have it right at hand, right now, during transition periods and when a missionary has first arrived in the field or in a new area.

Kits would best be kept in sturdy cloth, vinyl, or leather zippered cases (similar to what scriptures are kept in), of varying sizes and colors. This makes them easy to identify as the weeks and months go by. "The black container is my First Aid Kit." "The red zippered binder holds my Vital Documents." "The brown vinyl case is my Spares Kit."

It is better if the containers are larger than smaller to allow for items to be added to them as the mission progresses. If there is a "handle" at one end of the case, it makes it that much easier to grab and use.

The kits are listed in order of importance but the items in each kit are listed in alphabetical order for ease in reviewing and preparing. As before, this section is written to the parents.

❑ First Aid Kit.

A simple, but complete First Aid Kit will add comfort and capacity to your missionary's first days and weeks in the field. He or she will come to this source often for alleviating pain, discomfort, and to bind up burst blisters.

Organize for a Mission

- Alcohol (to clean wounds)
- Antibiotic Ointment
- Anti-fungal Ointment (especially for humid climates)
- Anti-itch Ointment

A Sister who served in South America says: "One of the more important things I needed on my mission was lotion TO STOP THE ITCH FROM BUG BITES. I would recommend insect repellent, too."

- Band-Aids
    - ☐ *Band-Aids of varying sizes and shapes*
    - ☐ *Butterfly closure bandaid (for holding deeper cuts closed) until professional medical attention can be received*
- Cold Medications
- Cotton Balls (to clean wounds)
- Fever Medications
- Hydrocortisone Cream (for skin ailments)
- Insect Repellent (if appropriate to the mission)
- Nail clippers, two sets each of fingernail clippers and toenail clippers. In addition to having fingernails nicely trimmed, it will be important to have toenails nicely squared off a little past the end of the toe to avoid ingrown

toenails. A sturdy toenail clipper does this job nicely.

A Sister adds an interesting insight: "I kept a pair of baby nail clippers on my key chain for hangnails, so I had it with me at all times."

One pair of nail clippers and one pair of toenail clippers go into the Spares Kit (see page 141) because these are often not available in some areas and the spares will really come in handy if your missionary has misplaced his or her first set of clippers.

- Pain Medications
- Prescriptions

Send as much as is allowable of your missionary's medications if they are going to a place where getting prescriptions will be difficult, lengthy, or of questionable quality.

Send sufficient to get them started on their mission if they will be able to refill their prescriptions during the 18 to 24 months of service.

Missionaries should take all preventive medications prescribed while at the Missionary Training Center and supplied by their mission president during the mission. In addition, they also need to take additional medications received from their mission president (before they return home) that are to be

Organize for a Mission

taken afterwards. This will provide long-term health protection.

- Q-tips
- Thermometer (in a protective case)
- Tweezers (the best you can find and afford)
- Vitamins

❑ Office Kit.

While the First Aid Kit comforts the missionary, the Office Kit enables him or her to function at a higher level. Of all the kits my missionaries took, the Office Kit was the one other missionaries borrowed most from because office supplies made it possible to keep their lives neat, their schedules workable, and their paperwork organized.

- Calculator. Solar/battery combination is best. Get a simple calculator that will add, subtract, multiple, and divide.

- Purchase an extra set of calculator batteries. These are kept in Spares Kit (see page 141).

- Corkboard Pins (stored in small, sturdy container). This will allow your missionary to hang pictures, phone lists, and other important information near his or her desk area.

Preparation of Essential Kits

- Envelopes (for mailing letters). This is in addition to the writing materials your missionary has purchased for his or her use during the Missionary Training Center.

- Glue sticks. This will help your missionary begin putting his or her treasured paperwork into journals.

- Mailing Labels (with your permanent home address). This is an important addition that will keep packages and letters that are mailed home by your missionary arriving at the right address.

- Paper Clips (stored in small sturdy container). A paper clip container with a hole surrounded by a magnet at the top of the container enables the simple movement of a finger to retrieve a paper clip.

- Paper Punch. This tool allows your missionary to punch, organize, and store letters from home, papers received during the mission, and other documents in a binder. This process of punching and storing will keep important papers safe and secure during his or her travels.

- Pens, Pencils, and Pencil Sharpener.

- Post-it Notes (or pads of scratch paper).

- Rubber Bands (stored in small ziploc bag).

- Ruler.

- Permanent Marking Pens. These should be purchased in both black ink (for writing on light items) and silver ink (for writing on dark surfaces). Thin and thick-lined pens make it easier to write on different-sized surfaces. These tools will also aid in labeling mission field acquisitions.

- Scissors, Paper.

- Stamps. Missionaries are requested to bring two or more stamps to the Missionary Training Center. Send additional stamps, as needed, for mailing written letters home during the missionary's stay at the Missionary Training Center. After his or her arrival at the actual mission field, additional postage, in the amounts and kinds appropriate for the locality, can then be purchased for sending letters or packages home.

    Stamps are best put in a small, well-built, easy-to-recognize container and kept in the Office Kit so they will not "get lost" in the chaos.

- Stationery. It is best if this stationery is of a standard size (8.5" x 11" is best for long-term journal storage in the "Stay-At-Home Missionary" Journals), of good quality (20-pound paper or better), and three-hole punched. If it is lined, it is easier to write upon. These hard-copy letters, after they are received from the missionary, can be easily kept in chronological order in the "Stay-At-Home" Missionary Journals. See page 205 for further details.

Again, missionaries should leave adequate margins around the edges of each sheet of stationery so the three-hole punching doesn't destroy his or her writing.

- Tape. Both single-sided and double-sided Scotch tape will accommodate many different needs during the mission.

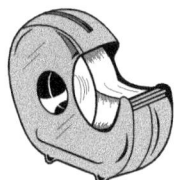

❑ Cooking Kit.

Missionaries begin to cook almost immediately upon their arrival in the mission field proper. Having the necessary tools to measure correctly ensures a smoother transition until local practices can be learned and cookbooks read (especially if the cookbooks are in a foreign language or use a different measuring method).

- Measuring spoons and cups. This will make it easier to use any recipes that are sent from home.

- A conversion table is handy when measuring spoons and cups don't exactly fit the need.

A Sister missionary shares: "If you go overseas, there will be a different measuring system so 'homeland' measuring cups could be helpful. Because we did not have these, we managed to figure out conversions or we improvised."

❑ Recipe Box.

Make up several recipe cards of your family's favorite, easy meals. Sometimes the ingredients won't be available in the mission field, but it is better to have the recipes than not, especially if your son or daughter is going to a foreign mission where reading even simple recipe instructions will be nearly impossible for a significant period of time because of possible language barriers.

Not willing to learn much about cooking before his mission and not knowing exactly what he would face during the first week in the mission field, one of our sons purchased hot dogs for one of his dinners. But not knowing precisely how to cook them and finding that the pans stored under the apartment sink were covered with unknown and probably unsanitary particles, he ate cold hot dogs for his first dinner and then washed and stored the pans in a cleaner environment, asked around about cooking hot dogs, and wrote home for more complete cooking instructions.

☐ Repair Kit.

Almost as important as the First Aid Kit items are those that will help the missionary repair and fix items while on his or her mission. Think carefully about your missionary's past experience, use of repair items, and any potential needs you can foresee. Having a bit of this and little of that makes it easier to hold things together until professionals can be called or a purchase made. Some possible items to consider include:

- Tape
  - ☐ *Duct tape*
  - ☐ *Masking tape*
  - ☐ *Packing tape*

A Sister explains: "Bring duct tape. There were so many times I wished that we had duct tape. I know that sounds funny, but I would give any missionary duct tape as a going away gift."

- Set of miniature screwdrivers (the kind for fixing reading glasses)

- Larger screwdriver with different sizes and kinds of heads (regular and Phillips)

- Pair of small pliers

☐ Sewing Kit.

You will facilitate missionary's clothing maintenance and care if a complete Sewing Kit is prepared for their use. Possible items include:

- Patches and matching thread. 4" x 4" pieces of fabric matching (as nearly as possible) the pants, skirts, jumpers, vests, jackets, blouses, and shirts taken on the mission should be gathered and put into a ziploc bag along with small, matching spools or bobbins of thread. These can then be used for mending.

Our first son tore the leg of his pants on an exposed box spring during his first day in the mission field. This happened before I understood the importance of sending patches along so he used his suitcase handle cover to help patch his pants, as he had no other available fabric. My other, subsequent missionaries all got patches of fabric and matching thread!

- Spare buttons that match those of the clothing going on the mission should be taken along for the smaller emergencies of life. These can be kept in a small ziploc bag along with matching thread.

- Thin yarn matching both socks and sweaters can be used for mending. While it is likely your missionary will purchase more socks before he or she will sit down and mend them, circumstances sometimes lend themselves to mending, especially if a sweater comes unraveled. It is better to help them be prepared.

Preparation of Essential Kits

I purchased this yarn in the craft section of my local store where it comes in many colors for cross-stitching and crewelwork. A small skein of each needed color will usually be enough for the mission.

- Two larger, blunt-ended needles to mend socks and sweaters

- Smaller, sharp-ended needles to mend shirts, blouses, skirts, jumpers, and pants

- Egg, wooden

I purchased wooden eggs at a craft store (about the size of a real egg) that I painted white and added to our sons' sewing kits. They put this "egg" inside their shirt or under their pants just at the hole to hold the fabric or weave taunt while they mended. It created a stable surface against which to poke the needle.

- Safety pins in a goodly number from "miniature" to "diaper" sizes should be chosen. They can and will be used for any number of reasons during the mission. They should be kept in a small, sturdy container.

- Scissors (small sewing) should be sharp, easy to handle, and of higher quality. It is best if the sharp end is sheathed when stored to keep unknowing fingers from being punctured.

Our first missionary son found his sewing scissors to be invaluable in many different situations and was glad they were of the highest quality because they got used for a lot more than cutting fabric, including opening boxed milk cartons.

- Straight pins for holding fabric during a mending session (preferably stored by sticking them into a pin cushion) can then be stored in a sturdy container. These should be longer pins with plastic, colored heads for ease in seeing them both on the item being mended and when they accidentally fall to the floor.

❏ Shoeshine Kit.

Because a missionary's appearance is so vital both to their self-esteem and their capacity to influence those they approach during missionary work, a Shoeshine Kit is essential. These tools should be kept in ziploc bags to keep them clean and to keep other items in a missionary's suitcase, drawer, or shelf from becoming stained. The Shoeshine Kit might contain:

- Shoe polish. This should be in all the colors of your missionary's shoes and boots.

- Shoe horn. This will make is easier to get shoes on and off, especially when they are new. It will considerably lengthen the life of shoes and boots as the rear area of footwear will tend to stay straight and sturdy with the use of a shoehorn.

- Shoe cloth and brush. Send the necessary shoe polish cloths and/or brushes to keep shoes and other footwear in tiptop condition because part of looking like a missionary is having polished footwear. People will notice shoes almost right away as they evaluate your missionary personally and listen to his or her message. Footwear needs special and continued attention if missionaries are to look their best at all times.

- Waterproofing paste, gel, and spray. See "Waterproofing Paste, Gel, and Spray" on page 116 for additional footwear care information.

Shoes and boots should be well polished and/or waterproofed frequently to maintain and protect the leather. While the "express" shoeshine disposables are useful for quick and easy upkeep, they are not a substitute for careful caring of shoes, one of the larger mission investments.

❏ Spares Kit.

As much as possible, choose items to send on the mission that take the same size and kind of batteries. This will facilitate using the same batteries for several different needs, which simplifies any missionary's life. In some circumstances, it would be

Organize for a Mission

appropriate to take a charger and rechargeable batteries.

- Alarm clock batteries
- Calculator batteries
- Camera batteries
- Digital camera memory card(s)
- Fingernail and toe nail clippers
- Flashlight batteries
- Flashlight bulb
- Insoles (if you purchased footwear which has insoles)
- Shoelaces
    - ❑ Six or more spare sets for dress shoes.
    - ❑ One or two spare sets for tennis shoes. You can't send too many spares of these small, lightweight items.
- Watch batteries

❑ Vital Documents Kit.

Lost paperwork can be a devastatingly difficult situation, let alone time consuming for any missionary. How much easier to have a second, spare copy of all important documents gathered and stored in the missionary's possession. Such documents might include:

- Copy of birth certificate

- Copy of driver's license (this is in addition to the original license which the missionary carries with him or her)

- Copy of mission call

- Copy of passport (this is in addition to the original which the missionary carries on him or her)

- Copy of patriarchal blessing

- Copy of immunization records

Another copy of these vital documents should be kept at home for possible "resending" in an emergency. Keep these copies together behind the "Information" tab in the "Mission Preparations" Binder for easy retrieval. See "When the Mission Call Comes, Go to Work", page 10.

❑ Comfort Kit.

During the first weeks of a mission, items of comfort alleviate homesickness, tend to increase endurance, and just plain make it easier to keep going. Each mission field has certain items that are hard to find and which would be best sent in small quantities for the missionary's use either initially and/or later as a care package. These might include:

- Peanut butter or other delicacies not readily available in some localities.

- Maple syrup extract (used to make maple syrup, not readily available in some countries and delicious on missionary-made pancakes).

- A sentimental item or two. Consider tucking something particularly special in your missionary's suitcases for him or her to discover once they are in the Missionary Training Center.

For instance, I hand paint small wooden houses as a hobby. When our first missionary was sent off, I made up four of them, and tucked one in his luggage to be discovered some time into his mission experience. He indicated later he got out the wooden house at the beginning of each transfer to remember the trust we had in his work ethic, service, and diligence to his call. I subsequently hid the other three wooden houses in each of the other missionary's suitcases as their luggage was packed and they left for their labors. For each son, this painted house reminded him of our support!

❏ A Note About Labeling.

When all the shopping, gathering, and setting aside are done, it is extremely important to label everything that is going on the mission. This not only simplifies and clarifies which items are whose, it also helps when things get misplaced in the apartment, while living with several other missionaries, and when traveling from here to there. It just pays to label!

Whenever possible, the complete name of the missionary should be written on their personal possessions. If the whole name cannot be written, write the initials. For instance, Jane Susan Ashby would be written "jsa." It is useful to label possessions twice, once in a public place and again in a private place. For example, label a camera on the exterior and also on the interior for double safety. Then, if the first labeling becomes faded or smeared, an interior part of the possession can still prove ownership.

"Seek not to declare my word, but first seek to obtain my word, and then shall your tongue be loosed; then, if you desire, you shall have my Spirit and my word, yea, the power of God unto the convincing of men." D&C 11:21

Preparation of Essential Kits Checklist

☐ First Aid Kit.
- Alcohol
- Antibiotic Ointment
- Anti-fungal Ointment
- Anti-itch Ointment
- Band-Aids
- Cold Medications
- Cotton Balls
- Fever Medications
- Hydrocortisone Cream
- Insect Repellent
- Nail Clippers, Fingernail
- Nail Clippers, Toe
- Pain Medications
- Prescriptions
- Q-tips
- Thermometer
- Tweezers
- Vitamins

☐ Office Kit.
- Calculator
- Corkboard Pins
- Envelopes (for mailing letters)
- Glue Sticks
- Mailing Labels
- Paper Clips
- Pencils and Sharpener
- Pens
- Post-it Notes (or small pads of scratch paper)
- Rubber Bands

Preparation of Essential Kits Checklist
(continued)

- Permanent Marking Pens
- Scissors, Paper
- Stamps
- Stationery
- Tape, Scotch

☐ Cooking Kit.
- Measuring Spoons and Cups
- A Conversion Table

☐ Recipe Box.
- Recipe Cards

☐ Repair Kit.
- Tape, Duct
- Tape, Masking
- Tape, Packing
- Miniature Screwdrivers
- Larger Screwdriver (with various heads)
- Small Pliers

☐ Sewing Kit.
- Patches & Matching Thread
- Spare Buttons & Thread
- Thin Yarn
- Two Larger, Blunt-ended Needles
- Smaller, Sharp-ended Needles
- Egg, Wooden
- Safety Pins
- Scissors, Small Sewing
- Straight Pins

Organize for a Mission

Preparation of Essential Kits Checklist
(continued)

- ☐ Shoeshine Kit.
    - Shoe Polish
    - Shoe Horn
    - Shoe Cloth
    - Shoe Brush

- ☐ Spares Kit.
    - Alarm Clock Batteries
    - Calculator Batteries
    - Camera Batteries
    - Camera Memory Card
    - Flashlight Batteries
    - Flashlight Bulb
    - Insoles (if footwear was purchased which has insoles)
    - Nail Clippers, Fingernail (second set)
    - Shoelaces, Tennis Shoe
    - Shoelaces, Dress Shoes
    - Watch Batteries

- ☐ Vital Documents Kit.
    - Copy of Birth Certificate
    - Copy of Driver's License
    - Copy of Mission Call
    - Copy of Passport
    - Copy of Patriarchal Blessing
    - Copy of Shot Records

- ☐ Comfort Kit.
    - Peanut Butter
    - Maple Syrup Extract
    - Sentimental Item(s)

What You Need From Home

"This is my glory, that perhaps I may be an instrument in the hands of God to bring some soul to repentance; and this is my joy." Alma 29:9

Sharing part of yourself will be an important everyday activity of missionary work. Bring a few items that will not only help you get to know others, but which will make you comfortable in new and different settings. As before, this section is written directly to missionaries!

❑ Pictures.

Pictures of you, your family, and your home will greatly help as you become better acquainted with investigators, make friends with members, and share stories with those you meet. You might want to consider sending close-ups of people as this allows others to get a better feel of personalities and age.

- A recent photo of your immediate family

- Your home or a picture of your community (preferably a representative scene, such as snow-capped mountains or city skyscrapers)

- Yourself as a child (which will endear you to the many children you will meet) or an older photo of your more *complete* family if it includes members who have passed away.

I sent a photo of our family before our youngest son passed away from leukemia. This proved to be one of the most frequently used pictures because our missionaries could talk about tragedies, death, and the resurrection from a personal point of view as they shared this picture and their own testimony.

- You and your friends (group picture including you)

- Your local temple or church building

- Extended family including grandparents, if possible, which will endear the missionary to the older people.

These pictures should all be laminated and should be small enough to fit nicely in a wallet, so they are readily available to share with potential investigators, members, and fellow missionaries.

In addition, you may want to have another collection of small, personal photos to share with companions and other close mission friends.

Please do not bring any pictures that will be inappropriate for missionary work, as this will distract from your capacity to stay focused.

A Sister advises: "I would also recommend taking a small photo album with about 15 additional photos to share with companions and good friends during your mission."

❏ Pillow.

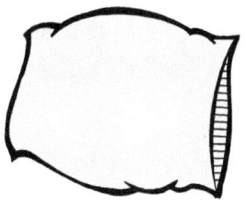

While you may bring any of several personal items from home, taking your own pillow will make all new surroundings more endurable because at least your "head" will feel at home every night.

❏ Something Very Personal.

There are probably several family traditions that would best be continued even while you are gone. Think carefully, plan accordingly, and plan to pack this item along with the others in your luggage.

Because it was traditional to give homemade crocheted slippers to our sons as Christmas gifts each year, two pairs of new slippers went into the luggage for the two Christmases they would be away from home. If you share your creativity regularly with your children, you may also want to plan and prepare these treasures accordingly.

"They had been taught by their mothers, that if they did not doubt, God would deliver them."
Alma 56:47

What You Need From Home Checklist

☐ Pictures.

- A recent photo of your immediate family
- Yourself as a younger child
- An older photo of your more *complete* family if it includes members who have passed away
- You and your friends
- Your local temple or church building
- Your extended family including grandparents (if possible)
- Your home or a picture of your community
- Other appropriate photos to share

☐ Pillow.

☐ Something Very Personal.

Packing For Easier Travel

"I will go before your face. I will be on your right hand and on your left, and my Spirit shall be in your hearts, and mine angels round about you, to bear you up." D&C 84:88

Traveling anywhere while handling heavy pieces of luggage, a carry-on bag, and items tucked in suits or a smaller bag can be very daunting for any missionary. Much consideration must be taken when purchasing luggage and/or missionary items and then packing them for travel. Several important questions must be addressed and so this section is written to parents.

❑ Will it all fit in the luggage?

Before purchasing luggage, check into the dimensional limitations for each piece of luggage and the individual luggage weight limits with the airport(s) from which your missionary will be traveling.

It is useful to have a pre-pack session several days before the final packing. It so much easier to make hard decisions without the stress of time limits, so consider having one "practice" packing session before they feel pressed for time.

In addition, a professional clothier suggests taking all clothing out of its original wrappings, removing all price tags, and discarding all clips and pins to facilitate getting more items in the luggage, plus saving time and forestalling a lot of trash at the Missionary Training Center. Also, items left in their original wrappings are often charged import duty when going through a foreign country's customs. Thus, the missionary traveling to a foreign Missionary Training Center would do well to have his or her luggage items "personalized."

❑ Will it weigh too much for air travel and there will be heavy penalties?

This is such an important consideration for missionaries traveling by air. Remember, that in addition to the items taken to the Missionary Training Center, about eight to twelve pounds of additional materials

Packing for Easier Travel

will be received at the Missionary Training Center. Both space and weight allowance should be made for this additional need if the missionary is traveling a second time by air to his or her mission field assignment.

I have been in more than one airport watching sad and distraught missionaries unloading items from their suitcases, wondering what to remove because their luggage was severely overweight. Yes, you can pay for the extra poundage, but it is very expensive. And besides, missionaries are going to have to move that weight around each and every time he or she is transferred, plus any additional weight as they pick up treasures, gifts, and mementos from their mission. It is better to initially travel with a bit less weight and bulk whenever possible!

One of our sons watched a fellow missionary pay a steep fee to bring home overly heavy luggage. The fee cost more than the newly purchased "gifts" were worth, but the circumstances and time restrictions made it easier to pay than to unpack, decide what to take out, and repack his suitcase.

A good scale to calculate your weight, a little practice at packing, and a lot of "just leave it out" will make what is taken worth the cost and the effort. Generally, if it's a tool, it goes in, if it's a trinket, it doesn't!

❑ Can the missionary handle all the luggage pieces alone?

A professional clothier suggests using an "even pull" technique when moving luggage. Haul the largest and usually heaviest piece of luggage with one hand. "Piggyback" the second and third pieces together and pull them with the other hand to even out the weight and bulkiness while moving from place to place.

A Sister shares: "Get luggage you can easily carry around, not too big and not too many pieces. Some missionaries had two bigger bags and a small carry-on. Luggage that hooks together is really handy. I didn't bring a carry-on bag, which was nice when I was transferred because it was one less bag to carry, but a pain when we had to stay overnight at someone else's apartment for Zone Conference. You just have to choose your battles.

"I would always recommend smaller luggage. Don't carry too much around. Throw away stuff you don't need; it is just a pain when you transfer and have to carry huge suitcases in buses and trains."

Another Sister comments: "Suitcase space is very limited and valuable. I barely fit everything in my suitcase before going to the Missionary Training Center not realizing I would be getting a bunch of books and mission materials that I would have to also fit in. I ended up sending some things home to be able to fit everything else in my suitcases.

"Keep in mind you'll need to be able to carry/roll all of your luggage yourself through airports, train stations, subways, and from the bus stop."

❑ **If flying, have liquids, sharp objects, or other restricted items been removed from carry-on bags, purses, and pockets?**

In all of the excitement, don't forget the air travel regulations that restrict certain types of items. This is one time you will be glad if you make careful plans beforehand.

❑ **Initial trip to Missionary Training Center.**

If going to the Provo, Utah Missionary Training Center, certain documents need to be handy and therefore should be kept secured in the missionary's clothing.
These include:

- Driver's License or Photo Identification Card
- Immunizations/Preventive Medication Requirements Form
- Passport
- Temple Recommend
- Visa

Other items should be convenient but secured in your missionary's luggage. This will allow one last review of items that would be difficult to replace or purchase after your missionary leaves home.

When traveling, remember that important or vital documents should *not* be kept in the outside zippered pockets of luggage where they are more exposed. All luggage should be well *labeled inside and out* with complete contact information (including the missionary's home address) to facilitate easy retrieval and possible return in the eventuality they become lost.

If traveling to an overseas Missionary Training Center, missionaries should carry Missionary Training Center contact information and instructions of what to do and whom to call upon arrival at the foreign destination. This information is in the Missionary Packet or should be received from the mission president. If someone is not there to meet your missionary, it is helpful to have this contact information very handy in what will be an otherwise confusing situation.

❑ Packing During the Mission Field Experience.

In addition to the initial trip to the Missionary Training Center, missionaries travel occasionally for District and/or Zone Conferences and splits with other missionaries. There will be additional travel during transfers and possible overnight stays at the mission home. Learning to pack quickly, compactly, and also to live out of a suitcase will greatly enhance the missionary experience. There will likely to be more than one occasion when your missionary will have just a few hours' notice to pack up and be ready to go. The missionary should pack so that alikes are kept together.

Items that can be used even though they are wrinkled (such as night clothing and underwear) can be rolled and packed together in a slightly larger bag to facilitate more organized travel. It will also save many a dig through the suitcase for the toiletries bag or the right pair of shoes if these items are grouped and kept in the same place each and every time they pack.

Generally, skills for packing make logical sense. Put small, heavier objects such as books, journals, and papers in the smaller suitcase. Put bulkier, lighter items such as clothes, coats, and shoes in the larger suitcase. Cover all items that might soil other items in the luggage. Always put heavier items in the area of the suitcase that will be at the bottom during travel. Put lighter items near the area of the suitcase that will be at the top during travel.

Put smaller items inside bigger items to save space. For instance, socks can be put into shoes, scarves and gloves in the middle of hangers, and belts inside boots. Enclose fragile items inside a sturdy container using some kind of additional packaging. This will help more fragile items survive from one transfer to another. Lastly, put toiletry items, underwear, and nighttime needs in a mission bag or a backpack for easy retrieval while traveling or when first arriving at the next destination, as this makes missionary journeys easier.

Organize for a Mission

Packing For Easier Travel Checklist

Questions to be asked:

- ☐ Will it all fit in the luggage?
- ☐ Will it weigh too much for air travel and there will be heavy penalties?
- ☐ Can your missionary handle all the luggage pieces alone?
- ☐ If flying, have liquids, sharp objects, or other inappropriate items been removed from the carry-on bags, purses, and pockets?

- ☐ Documents for Local Missionary Training Center.
  - Immunizations/Preventive Medication Requirements Form (often found in the Missionary Packet)
  - Driver's License or Photo Identification Card
  - Passport
  - Temple Recommend
  - Visa

- ☐ Information and Documents for Foreign Missionary Training Center.
  - Contact Information for Missionary Training Center (and instructions of what to do and whom to call, if necessary, upon arrival at the foreign destination)
  - Immunizations/Preventive Medication Requirements Form
  - Driver's License or Photo Identification Card
  - Passport
  - Temple Recommend
  - Visa

Starting Out Right, Right Away

"*Missionary work is hard, and full-time missionaries must be in good physical condition to serve... It is important to be able to read, speak, and write with intelligence... Learn how to study... Consistently and regularly read from the* Book of Mormon... *Start now to prepare for a full-time mission by adopting the appearance of a full-time missionary.*" Elder L. Tom Perry, November 2007 *Ensign*, page 48

Being a missionary will take a lot of focus, energy, and drive. There are important habits and skills that can serve you well, especially if they become or are already a regular part of your everyday routine. If it hasn't happened yet, work at these preparations now so you can focus on the many other new and interesting events during your missionary experience.

While this chapter is directed to missionaries, it is often helpful if parents also participate in acquiring and practicing these personal habits and skills. It makes it more fun for everyone, keeps the routines happening, and helps to motivate the missionary!

❑ Personal Habits.

Begin using an alarm clock now and (as nearly as possible) get up and go to bed on missionary time. It will be that much easier when you get to the Missionary Training Center. There will rarely be time for too much sleep for the next eighteen months to two years, so begin to discipline yourself now. It will just make it easier when you enter the mission field.

A missionary wrote home that sometimes he craved sleep more than anything else during the first few months of his mission. It was not that he had slept longer than needful during his later teenage years, but he had been less than disciplined in getting up at the same time each morning. As this skill came more naturally to him, he learned to handle other difficult, missionary skills with greater ease.

One of our sons wished he had slept on the couch or taken a nap on the floor for an hour because all those sleeping positions were part of his mission experience.

Make your bed and neat your side of the bedroom each and every morning! It is a small, but important way to gain control of this part of your life and increase your "personal orderliness."

❑ Exercise Habits.

A mission will be one of the more rigorous experiences of your life. Begin now to get some good, long exercise each and every day. This is what missionary work is all about: "Each and every day." Your stamina will increase, as will your skill to focus on language and memorization skills. When your body is functioning at a place of high capacity, so can your mind.

❑ Grooming Habits.

One important way to prepare for missionary service is to begin grooming and dressing appropriate to mission standards whether in casual or more formal wear. Much of your confidence upon entering the Missionary Training Center will be due to your well-established grooming habits.

Elders: While it is possible you will receive a second haircut upon your arrival to meet Missionary Training Center guidelines, getting a missionary hair cut right after your call will "move" you towards a mission. Shorter hair that is still long enough to part and comb, evenly tapered, with sideburns above the middle of the ear are the standards to follow. It can help you to feel and act like a missionary right away.

Organize for a Mission

One of the Missionary Training Center surprises for several of our sons was the advice to get an additional hair trim after their admission. No matter what haircut you believe is short enough, be prepared for a different opinion and respond accordingly!

Sisters: You will want an easy-to-maintain hairstyle that won't cover your missionary nametag. Get a good haircut right away. This will allow you time to fuss, experiment, and maybe even change your mind about hairstyles before entering the Missionary Training Center.

Keep your hair clean and neatly combed. How many times a day does your hair need to be combed to stay looking neat? Begin practicing now, maybe combing it each time you visit the rest room or brush your teeth.

How many times a week does your hair need to be washed to look attractive? Make that a part of your routine this week and every week until you leave.

Keep your fingernails clean and neatly trimmed. In addition to your general grooming, fingernails are observed as part of initial impressions about you and your message. Keep them neatly cut and presentable!

Neating up the bathroom every time you use it will make for a more peaceful time at home now, with your companions later, and will set a good example for newer missionaries with which you serve.

❑ Obedience Habits.

To follow mission rules later, begin following all rules at home NOW! It will make it easier and you will be far more spiritually safe.

One missionary in our area, thinking he would circumvent his parent's specific instructions about NO ice skating on the eve of his departure, severely broke his ankle which delayed his entrance into the Missionary Training Center by six weeks and encumbered the first part of his mission experience. It is not worthwhile to be less than totally committed to obedience.

While every mission has its own particular culture and imperatives, learning to be obedient and standing up against less eager Elders and Sisters will earn you a reputation as someone who is a "straight arrow" (if they are describing you nicely as a missionary who keeps each and every rule) and some less desirable terms (if they are being unkind). However, a great mission is laid upon the foundation of obedience, even in the small things, when under the tutelage of your mission president. Take care to listen and obey your parents now, your Missionary Training Center leaders during your training, and your mission president for the rest of the time! ALWAYS!

❑ Reading Habits.

Learning to read for a considerable period of time with great concentration is a skill to be practiced before the mission begins. Begin reading for a few minutes each day the scriptures and other good books like *Preach My Gospel*. Start with a timer and train yourself to stay at this task for longer and longer periods of time each day. This reading habit might best be started on Sundays and then added to your daily routine as your schedule and priorities allow.

❑ Social Skills.

Begin to say hello to more of the people you meet on the street, in the classroom, at work, or when shopping. This makes it much easier to be self-assured and fearless when you actually proselyte. Pull yourself out of your comfort zone just a bit initially and then as far as you can stretch once your confidence grows.

After being introduced to someone, use that person's name often while conversing with him or her. This will not only help you remember their name later, but it will make it easier to learn new names as the circle of your friendships grow to include new companions, fellow missionaries, investigators, and members of the Church where you serve.

Watch for opportunities to go on splits with the local missionaries where you live. This will provide invaluable exposure to the routines of missionary work, door approaches, and visiting with members and investigators.

Pay attention to your table manners and eating habits. Do you eat with your mouth closed, waiting to speak until you have swallowed, say "thank you" at the end of the meal, and asked to be excused from the table when finished? You will probably astound your parents if you begin to incorporate these habits into your everyday routines and also impress any investigators or members whose homes you visit while in the field.

Also, it may surprise you just how many different, unusual and sometimes difficult-to-swallow foods your mission will bring to your mouth. One way to accommodate this adventure is to begin eating new and unfamiliar foods whenever you can. At home, try something different and difficult for dinner. A lot of salt, pepper, and fast swallowing usually helps. If you happen to eat out, order something new from the menu, just to improve this skill in your life.

❑ Budgeting Skills.

There will be a certain amount of money each month for your living expenses while you serve a mission. It may be distributed via an ATM card or another method, but there will only be so much.

Watching your expenses and recording them so you have some money left at the end of the month will make for a full stomach, the rent paid, and your personal needs met. Start now to write down when you spend money, how much you spend, and where you spend it.

❑ Shopping Skills.

Buy some foods each week that can be eaten almost "as is," such as peanut butter, raisins, oatmeal, canned meats, canned pork and beans, canned soups and whatever else is available. Having these foods in your diet now will be good practice. Then, the long missionary days will also end with some good nutrition despite having little or no time and/or energy to cook.

One skill I neglected to teach my son was how to take a certain amount of money and purchase food supplies for a week. The first week of his mission field experience was miserable because he bought too much of this, too little of that, and not nearly enough of "eat it as it is" foods.

He was too shy to ask for help, too "green" to understand the language, and too hungry to really care much by the end of that long week...

❏ Cooking Skills.

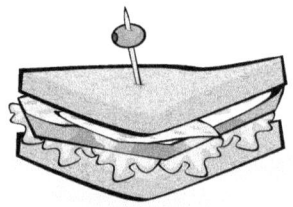

From the first day in the mission field, it is likely you will begin cooking. Learn to cook basic foods, as this will make those first days and weeks in the field more stomach friendly.

Practice cooking on a stove such items as:
- Rice
- Macaroni
- Noodles
- Spaghetti
- Potatoes
- Boiled eggs

Learn to fry in a pan:
- Pancakes
- French toast
- Fried and scrambled eggs
- Meat

Practice making a good, nutritious sandwich.

Learn to cook several, simple meals. While the ingredients will be unique to your particular mission, just learning to put a meal together greatly helps with the transition from home-cooked meals to being an able, independent cook in the mission field.

❑ Housecleaning Skills.

Generally there are four or more rooms and/or areas to clean during a mission: the living area, the kitchen, the bathroom, and the bedroom. These will be in different combinations depending on your situation. Sometimes they are all one room, sometimes four rooms or more, and sometimes they exist as areas in a few rooms. Whatever your comforts of life, there are specific tools and routines you can use when cleaning your abode to make this part of missionary life easier.

It is also likely you can plan on a "major" deep cleaning during the first week after any transfer, especially if the missionaries before you were slack in their cleanliness habits. Always clean up the apartment to meet your standards and leave it that way when you are later transferred. Nothing increases missionary's capacity quite like an orderly and clean abode.

Organize for a Mission

Begin now to neat and clean these four same rooms in your home or apartment so you are comfortable with these skills and they can come naturally to you in the mission field.

Bedroom	Bathroom
Kitchen	Living Area

❑ Bathroom.

Bathrooms are the hardest and the smelliest to clean (usually because they will have been neglected by previous missionaries). Several tools will be needed: Two cleaning cloths (washcloths or sponges), cleaner in a spray bottle, latex gloves, broom and dustpan, cup, and elbow grease.

- Pick up and discard in the wastebasket any unneeded items, toilet paper, facial tissue, and anything else that is cluttering the room but is no longer useful. Set aside items that need to be stored elsewhere.

Starting Out Right, Right Away

- Pick up any dirty clothes and put in the laundry basket. Return other misplaced items to their appropriate "homes."

- Pick up, take outside, and shake any rugs. Return them to the bathroom entry.

- Close vanity, drawers, and cupboard doors.

- Clean the mirror. Spray cleaner on the dry washcloth, wipe from top to bottom with side-to-side motions, until shiny and spotless.

- Clean the counter and sink. Spray counter and sink lightly with cleaning solution, wipe counters and taps with your now "damp" washcloth, wipe out and rinse sink.

- Wring out washcloth (which will now be your "wet" washcloth).

- Clean the tub/shower. Spray cleaner onto now wet washcloth; wipe down shower walls, crevices, taps, door and/or curtain from top to bottom with side-to-side motions. Rinse these same items with a cup and wring out wet washcloth. Shine taps with a "dry" washcloth.

- Clean the bathroom floor. Sweep the bathroom floor with a broom and dustpan. Discard the dirt in the wastebasket. Then wipe up the floor. This can be done by hand with the wet washcloth or with a wet mop and bucket of cleaning solution (which mop would be the same one used for cleaning other floors).

- Clean the toilet. Putting on latex gloves will make this less desirable, but very necessary task, more pleasant. Spray the toilet with cleaning solution, wipe down with wet washcloth. Clean toilet tank top, exterior, lid and seat (outside and in), rim, and bowl. Flush. Wipe again with the "damp" washcloth. Put down toilet lid.

- Confirm there is enough toilet paper on the roll for the next person's use and enough stashed nearby to last another week.

- Empty the wastebasket and reline with a plastic bag or paper sack.

- Return the bathroom rugs to their rightful place.

Starting Out Right, Right Away

- Put dirty washcloths or sponges in the laundry to be washed.

- Rinse the mop with clean water and put away (unless you are going to use it for another room).

❑ Kitchen.

<u>Kitchens</u> are the next most difficult room to clean. They are used regularly and get dirty quickly. Several tools will be needed: Two dry cleaning cloths (washcloths or sponges), cleaner in a spray bottle, a broom and dustpan, a mop, and more elbow grease.

- Clear dishes and other items from table and counters. Put dishes in dishwasher or a sink full of hot, soapy water. If hand washing, wash, rinse, dry and put away dishes.

- Put other items away in their rightful "homes."

- Pick up and discard in the wastebasket any unneeded items, paper goods, grocery bags, and anything else that is cluttering the room but is no longer useful.

- Pick up, take outside, and shake any rugs. Return them to the kitchen entry.

- Clean the counters, table, and other flat surfaces. Remove all items from the counters, table, and other flat surfaces and wipe them down with a dry washcloth that has been sprayed with cleaner. Shine with the second, dry washcloth.

- Clean kitchen chairs. Wipe chair backs, fronts, seats, and legs with the now "damp" washcloth.

- Clean the stove and/or microwave. Remove all items from the stove and put any removable stove parts in a sink of hot, soapy water to soak while you work. Wipe down the top of the stove, the front of the oven, the dials (where you turn on the stove) and any other parts that are sticky or dirty using the damp washcloth sprayed with cleaning solution. Wash, rinse off, and dry the removable stove parts and return them to their proper places on the stove.

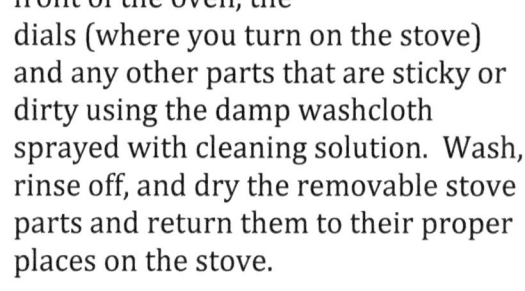

- Clean the refrigerator. Remove all items from the top of the refrigerator and wipe it off with the wet washcloth. Wipe down the front and sides of the refrigerator, too. Shine with the dry washcloth.

- Empty the refrigerator of all containers and discard any blue, green, or smelly items right away. Yuk! Wipe down the inside of the refrigerator with the same wet washcloth (rinsing it out in the soapy water in the sink as needed). Shine with the dry washcloth. (In some missions, the refrigerator will occasionally need defrosting.)

- Return the good food and condiments back to the refrigerator. Return appropriate items to the top of the refrigerator again.

- Clean the kitchen floor. Move any chairs aside. Sweep the floor with a broom and dustpan and discard the floor debris in the wastebasket. Then wipe up the floor. This can be done by hand on your knees with the wet washcloth or with a wet mop (which mop would be the same one used when cleaning other floors). Use hot soapy water in the sink to rinse the mop or washcloth as needed while cleaning the floor.

- Rinse the mop with clean water when the floor is done and put it away (unless you are going to use it for another room).

- Return chairs to their rightful places.

- Clean the sink. Empty out the dirty water and scrub the sink and taps with the wet washcloth. Shine the sink and taps with the dry washcloth.

- Empty the wastebasket and reline with plastic bag or paper sack.

- Return the kitchen rugs to their rightful place.

- Put used washcloths or sponges in the laundry to be washed.

❑ Bedroom.

The <u>bedroom</u> is almost the easiest area to clean. Several tools will be needed: Two clean, dry cleaning cloths (washcloths or sponges), cleaner in a spray bottle, a vacuum (if carpet), a broom/dustpan and mop/bucket of cleaning solution (if flooring), and plenty of elbow grease.

- Pick up and discard in the wastebasket any unneeded items, used scratch paper, broken objects, and anything else that is cluttering the room but is no longer useful.

- Pick up any dirty clothes and put in the laundry basket. Return other misplaced items to their appropriate "homes."

- Pick up, take outside, and shake any rugs. Return them to the bedroom entry.

- Open curtains or blinds to let in light.

- Close closet doors and drawers.

- Make the beds. This gives you neat, flat surfaces to put other items upon as you clean.
- Clear all items off from your study desk.

- Dust all flat surfaces with a dry washcloth including windowsill, chest of drawers, desk, chair, and lamp.

- Return the items to your study desk and arrange neatly. This order will help you focus when studying, writing, and planning.

- Sweep the floor or vacuum the carpet. Wipe up floor with a wet rag, if appropriate, or use the mop, if convenient.

- Return the bedroom rugs to their rightful place.

- Empty the wastebasket and reline with a plastic bag or paper sack.

- Put used washcloths or sponges in the laundry to be washed.

- Rinse the mop with clean water when the floor is done and put away (unless you are going to use it for another room).

❑ Living Area.

Clean the <u>living area</u>. This is usually the easiest area to clean because it is mostly just messy and dusty. Several tools will be needed: Two clean, dry cleaning cloths (washcloths or sponges), cleaner in a spray bottle, a mop and/or vacuum, and elbow grease.

- Pick up and discard any unneeded items, leftover food, unneeded containers, and anything else that is cluttering the room but is no longer useful.

- Pick up and put any dirty clothes in the laundry basket. Return all other misplaced items to their appropriate "homes."

- Straighten cushions on couches and chairs, articles on end tables, and items anywhere else.

- Open blinds/curtains.

- Remove and shake any rugs outside. Return to the entry of the living area.

- Dust all flat surfaces with dry washcloth that has been lightly sprayed with cleaner including windowsills, tables, lamps, and all other dusty surfaces.

- Clean the living area floor. If a hard surface floor, sweep with a broom and discard the floor debris in the wastebasket. Then wipe it up. This can be done by hand on your knees using a wet washcloth, or with a wet mop (which mop would be the same one used when cleaning other floors). If carpeted, vacuum thoroughly.

- Return the living area rugs to their rightful place.

- Empty the wastebasket and reline with plastic bag or paper sack.

- Put used washcloths or sponges in the laundry to be washed.

- Rinse the mop with clean water when the floor is done and put away. (It goes without saying, if you are cleaning the whole apartment, you would use the mop to clean the living area, kitchen, bath, and bedroom floor, rinsing as needed, and then clean it one last time after all the floors are done and put it away.)

Ordering and cleaning your "missionary world" in this way will give you confidence and comfort, plus be a pleasant place to stay when you return to your abode every night.

Detach, laminate, and fold in half the removable Missionary Cleaning Sheet on pages 183 to 186 to send along with your missionary. It has simple instructions for cleaning the four basic missionary apartment rooms. You may download, print, and laminate the Missionary Cleaning Sheets by going to *http://houseoforder.com/category/downloads/*.

Starting Out Right, Right Away

Missionary Clean a Bathroom!

- ☐ Several tools will be needed: Two clean, dry cleaning cloths (washcloths or sponges), cleaner in a spray bottle, latex gloves, broom and dustpan, cup, and elbow grease.
- ☐ Discard trash in the wastebasket
- ☐ Put all dirty clothes in laundry basket
- ☐ Shake rugs & leave outside bathroom door
- ☐ Put away all items:
    - o Put in their rightful place in bathroom or
    - o Put away in their rightful "home"
- ☐ Straighten towels
- ☐ Close vanity, drawers, and cupboard doors
- ☐ Clean mirrors with cleaning cloth
- ☐ Wipe down counters, clean sinks, and shine taps
- ☐ Scrub and rinse bathtub/shower, enclosure, and taps
- ☐ Shine bathtub/shower taps
- ☐ Sweep and wipe up/mop floor
- ☐ Clean toilet tank top, lid and seat (outside and in), exterior, rim, and bowl. Flush.
- ☐ Wipe outside of toilet with dry cleaning cloth and put down toilet lid
- ☐ Confirm there is enough toilet paper on roll
- ☐ Put cleaning cloths in the laundry basket
- ☐ Empty wastebasket, reline, & return to bathroom
- ☐ Return rugs and straighten

Organize for a Mission

Missionary Clean a Kitchen!

- ☐ Several tools will be needed: Two clean, dry cleaning cloths (washcloths or sponges), cleaner in a spray bottle, a broom and dustpan, a mop, and lots of elbow grease.
- ☐ Discard trash in the wastebasket
- ☐ Clear dishes and other items from table, counters, and top of frig:
    - o Put dishes sink full of hot water, wash and put away
    - o Put other items away in rightful "home"
- ☐ Shake rugs and leave outside kitchen door
- ☐ Wipe down table and counters
- ☐ Clean kitchen chair backs, fronts, seats, and legs
- ☐ Clean microwave and/or stove – wipe down exterior, dials, pans underneath stove elements
- ☐ Clean refrigerator – wipe front, sides, and top
- ☐ Empty the refrigerator and discard any blue, green, or smelly items right away. Yuk!
- ☐ Wipe down the inside of the refrigerator
- ☐ Return good food and condiments back to frig
- ☐ Move chairs, sweep and mop kitchen floor
- ☐ Clean mop and put away
- ☐ Push chairs in around the table
- ☐ Clean and dry sink and put cleaning cloths in the laundry basket
- ☐ Empty wastebasket, reline, and return to kitchen
- ☐ Return rugs and straighten

Starting Out Right, Right Away

Missionary Clean a Bedroom!

- [ ] Several tools will be needed: Two clean, dry cleaning cloths (washcloths or sponges), cleaner in a spray bottle, a vacuum (carpet), a broom & dustpan and mop bucket of cleaning solution (flooring), and more elbow grease.
- [ ] Discard trash in the wastebasket & empty it
- [ ] Put away all items:
    - Put in their rightful place in bedroom

    OR

    - Put away in their rightful "home"
- [ ] Put dirty clothes in laundry basket
- [ ] Shake rugs and leave outside bedroom door
- [ ] Make bed, open curtains, close doors & drawers
- [ ] Dust bedroom window sill, chest of drawers, desk, chair, lamp, and all other flat surfaces
- [ ] Arrange items neatly on desk
- [ ] Dry/wet mop floor and/or vacuum carpet
- [ ] Put cleaning cloths in the laundry basket
- [ ] Rinse the mop with clean water and put away
- [ ] Return rugs to rightful place

Organize for a Mission

Missionary Clean a Living Area!

- ❑ Several tools will be needed: Two clean, dry cleaning cloths (washcloths or sponges), cleaner in a spray bottle, a mop and/or vacuum, and elbow grease.

- ❑ Discard trash in the wastebasket

- ❑ Put away all items:
    - o Put in their rightful place in living area OR
    - o Put away in their rightful "home"

- ❑ Straighten cushions on couches and chairs, items on end tables, and anywhere else

- ❑ Open blinds/curtains

- ❑ Shake rugs and leave outside living area door

- ❑ Dust window sills, tables, lamps, and all other flat surfaces

- ❑ Dry/wet mop floor and/or vacuum carpet

- ❑ Empty the wastebasket, reline, and return to its rightful place

- ❑ Put washcloths or sponges in the laundry basket

- ❑ Return rugs to their rightful place

❑ Laundry Skills.

In some missions, laundry is done by machine either at the apartment or at a laundromat. Either way, missionaries will need to know simple techniques for getting the proper amount of soap and the right number of dirty clothes in the washing machine, how long the machine takes to do a load, and how the dryer works. Gain experience at home by doing your own laundry. It is also helpful to visit a local laundromat to experience doing your laundry in such an establishment.

In other missions, laundry is done by hand. This requires some patience, learning to wring clothes out by hand, and hanging items on a clothesline.

One of our sons did his laundry in five-gallon buckets. One bucket was for soaking and washing, another one for rinsing. Then the clothes were hand wrung and hung on an outdoor clothes line to dry for 24 hours or so (with the hope that the humidity was low enough they would actually get dry).

Another son, who went to Europe, ironed a clean shirt every morning for the duration of his mission as dryers were unknown and all laundry was dried on racks sitting around their apartment.

A third son who also hung his clothes on an outdoor line found that hanging his pants and socks inside out seemed to preserved their durability and kept them from fading so quickly.

❑ Ironing Skills.

In some missions, shirts and blouses are ironed every morning. If possible, have a capable friend or family member demonstrate how hot an iron should be for different fabrics and how to iron a shirt or blouse quickly and effectively. Easy instructions follow for the first-time ironer.

- First, (1A) lay the collar (back side up) on the ironing board and iron until smooth and flat. If your iron is too hot, this allows you to scorch an unseen surface first and then make necessary adjustments.

- Then, (1B) iron the front side of the collar.

- (2) Lift and hold the shirt or blouse by the lower, outside corners of the back yoke (that part of the shirt which covers the shoulder blades). Lay shirt or blouse on the ironing board and iron yoke. If there is no yoke, this step can be done when the main body of the item is being ironed (see instruction 5A below).

- (3A) If long-sleeved, lay one wristband out flat and iron. (3B) Then iron the second wristband.

- (4A) Lay one sleeve flat and iron. (4B) Then do the other one.

Starting Out Right, Right Away

- (5A) Lay the left front piece of the shirt or blouse on the ironing board (lengthwise, neckline to bottom) and iron. Move the shirt or blouse around on the ironing board to iron the (5B) left back, (5C) right back, and then (5D) right front.

- Hang shirt or blouse up carefully to cool down.

- Wear with humility and pleasure (as you ironed it yourself).

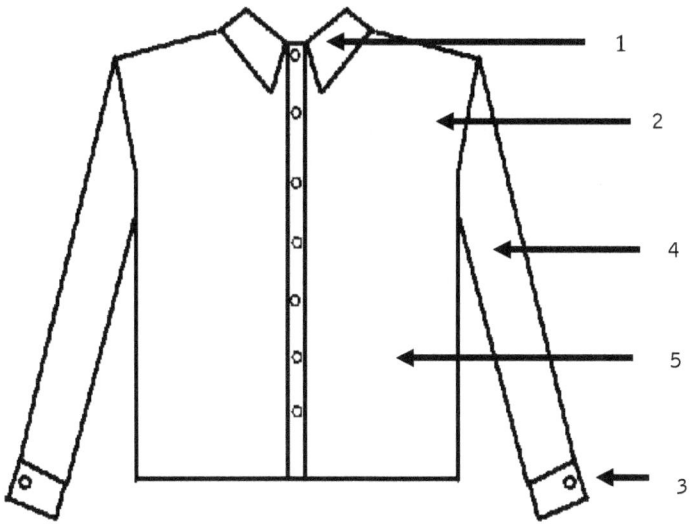

❑ Mending Skills.

Learn to thread a needle. This is no small task if you have never done it and is essential to all mending.

Learn to tie a knot at the end of both threads that have just been threaded through a needle. It is a simple, but important skill to roll the thread off your first finger and thumb (after winding it around your first finger) and get a knot that is clean and tight. This is best learned from someone who has hand sewn for sometime. Practice until you get good at it, as it will make all mending easier!

While most missionaries will purchase new socks if

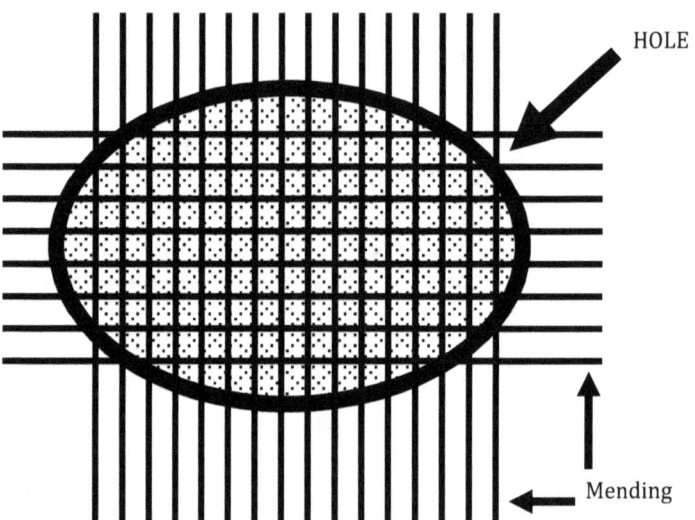

they are available, it is valuable to learn to mend small holes in socks to lengthen their use. This is a technique of threading matching yarn on a larger, blunt-end needle and hand sewing this yarn one way across the hole and then weaving the yarn up and down over the first yarns in the other direction over the hole until the hole is filled in. This skill can also be employed to mend small holes in woven clothing articles like sweaters and scarves.

Learn to mend an "L" shaped tear, a common mishap for mission field pants, skirts, shirts, and blouses. This is a technique of sewing matching thread over and then under as you work your way down and across the tear. It is helpful to hold a small piece of matching or near-matching fabric under the tear with straight pins to add stability to the mend as you do the hand sewing. You can trim off the excess "underneath" fabric patch with scissors after the mending is done.

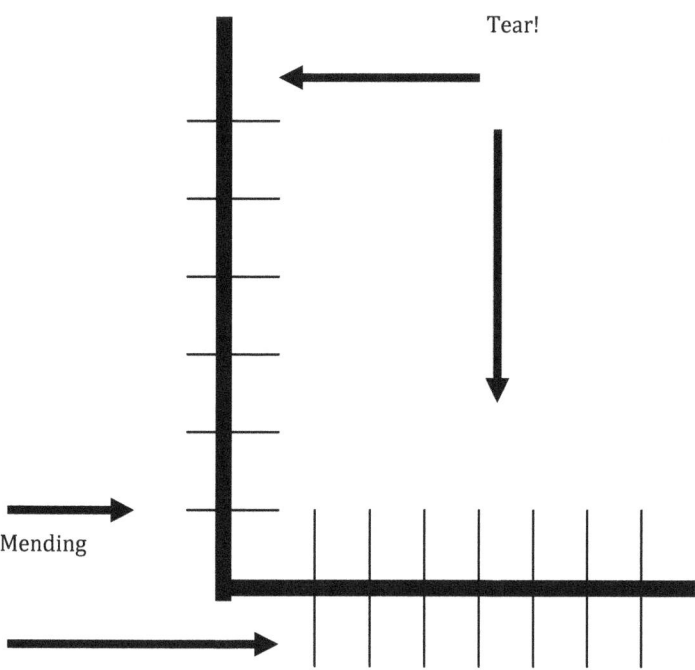

Learn to sew on a button. This is relatively easy once you have been shown how, but learn to do it well to make all such repairs more automatic when they need attention.

All these skills, learned and practiced before you leave will save time, stress, and allow you to serve other missionaries because you will be "the one that knows how!

Starting Out Right, Right Away Checklist

- ☐ Personal Habits.
- ☐ Exercise Habits.
- ☐ Grooming Habits.
- ☐ Obedience Habits.
- ☐ Reading Habits.
- ☐ Social Skills.
- ☐ Budgeting Skills.
- ☐ Shopping Skills.
- ☐ Cooking Skills.

   Practice cooking:
   - Rice
   - Pasta
   - Potatoes
   - Boiled eggs

   Learn to fry:
   - Pancakes
   - French toast
   - Fried and scrambled eggs
   - Meat

   Learn to make a sandwich.

   Learn to cook simple meals.

- ☐ Housecleaning Skills.
   - Bathroom
   - Kitchen
   - Bedroom
   - Living Area

Starting Out Right, Right Away Checklist
(continued)

- ❑ Laundry Skills.
- ❑ Ironing Skills.
- ❑ Mending Skills.

- ❑ Detach and laminate the removable Missionary Cleaning Sheets on pages 183 to 186 for use in the mission field.

What It Will Be Like

"[They] did suffer much, both in body and in mind, such as hunger, thirst and fatigue, and also much labor in the spirit... And the Lord said unto them... I will make an instrument of thee in my hands unto the salvation of many souls." Alma 17:5, 11

For The Missionary –

One of the strongest emotions after receiving a mission call is wonder at what it will be like. Searching, learning, asking around, and investigating will make all the difference in your basic knowledge and your confidence as you approach a mission. As mentioned before, investigate what returned missionaries have to say about the area where you will be serving. This can sometimes be done by finding the mission website, asking questions, and emailing returned missionaries.

They have been there and while you may not follow all their advice, it will give you an idea or two about how to prepare, what to expect, and the kinds of experiences they have had. Listen to several different missionaries so you can discern what is tongue-in-cheek advice and what counsel you can really follow.

One of the first big challenges for the missionary is saying goodbye to loved ones, family, and maybe even a close friend or two. It will not be easy, but usually shorter goodbyes are better than longer ones, sooner is better than later, and less  is better than more. No matter how much or how often you say goodbye, when you are in the Missionary Training Center, there will still be eighteen months to two years ahead. Be wise, be careful, and say goodbye with due care.

Emotions are likely to run especially raw on the day of your departure, whether your family takes you directly to the Missionary Training Center or drops you off at the airport or another transportation depot. You will be anxious to be gone and yet sad to be saying goodbye. This conflict is natural and you may find yourself more emotional than normal as you try to make sense of the excitement, anguish, and fear happening all at the same time.

And then suddenly it will be like you have never been anywhere else but the Missionary Training Center. Then when you enter the field, it will be like you have never been anywhere else but the mission field. Up/down, sad/happy, confused/calm, and bewildered/peaceful is the constant emotional background of a mission. It will happen over and over again as you move from one place to another, from one transfer to the next, from one area to another, and finally leave the mission field and travel back home again. Be patient with yourself. It is hard, but the discouraging moments won't last long if you get involved and focused on each new circumstance you encounter.

You will likely face several of the following situations during your mission. There will not be too much space for your personal items while in the mission field. This will mean using what "organization" skills you have or being creative once you arrive.

> *Only a small area was designated for all the personal items of one of our missionary sons during most of his mission.. Learning to keep things neat and organized made for an easier mission experience all around.*

Often, investigators will live in dwellings much "humbler" than any you have ever known existed. Keeping your own life simple now as you prepare will make it easier to be a "part of the people" that you serve.

You will have times when you are cold. Learning to layer clothing helps make the most of temperature differences from outside to inside, from windy to calm, from morning through afternoon and into the evening.

You will have times when you are very HOT! Again, layering will allow you to remove and add clothing with the temperature's fluctuation.

What It Will Be Like

> *Two of our sons joke there were many days when they searched for the shade of a telephone pole just to have a moment's respite from the heaviness of the hot sun.*

You will have times when you are sweaty. This is when a handkerchief comes in handy for wiping your face, neck, arms, and hands. You will have times when you are thirsty and will be very grateful for a proffered glass of water or another drink.

You will have times when you are hungry. If you struggle with your blood sugar, you might keep a small ziploc bag of food with you to munch on at all times. These snacks could be fixed on Preparation Day so they are readily available before each morning's departure.

You will have times when you need a restroom and there won't be much in the way of sanitary comforts.

> *One of our sons went to an area where latrines were simple holes in the ground. He quickly learned to carry a small, personal stash of facial tissue and/or toilet paper, just in case!*

There will be humorous times, too, like when you realize that the only safe place from critters is in the refrigerator. It will feel strange to store your toothbrush in there, but it makes for a better night's sleep.

There will be many a time when you will have to do what needs to be done even when you haven't the faintest idea about how to do it (like washing a tie because dry cleaning isn't possible, or cooking a new and different vegetable, or cleaning a toilet that isn't exactly the shape and size you have been used to in the past).

You will have times when you are very tired. You will learn to be awake longer than you ever thought possible. Other times you will crave sleep so much that between lying down at night and the alarm ringing in the morning seems but a small moment. Occasionally you will doze off on the bus, in a car, or even during a discussion (but try not to, as it doesn't help much with the conversion process).

> *As an Elder serving in the Orient wrote home about knowing when he was finally comfortable with his missionary surroundings: "There is less enduring a mission and more serving a mission."*

One of your several responsibilities will be to write an occasional letter to your family. This may take the form of an email or a hard copy letter (depending upon your current situation and mission rules). The letters should include specifics of your week's activities, details that others might find humorous or informative, and concrete points which will help those you love understand how it really, really is for you in the mission field. Keep away from, "It was a great week, I am doing fine, and we really walked a lot" and focus more on, "We got lost yesterday and with no one to understand me or my companion's barely acquired language skills, it took us about three hours (and inquiring at the butcher's, the baker's, and the furniture maker's) to get back on the right bus to return to our apartment. In the meantime, we met three new investigators!"

My last missionary son suggests not writing home about minor problems, insignificant companionship issues, and little illnesses because these challenges often unduly alarm parents and usually resolve themselves by the next letter. A small illness mentioned in one letter seems to blossom into a more dangerous situation in the mind of a "worried" mother before the next letter is received. And if the "illness" is not mentioned in the next letter, then the worrier worries more. Did it get better, is it worse, what is happening now? Keeping your letters upbeat and devoid of minor problems will make your mission easier and your parent's experience calmer.

You will also be taking pictures from time to time. If it is a particularly important event or place in your missionary experience, whether you are using a digital or film camera, take two or three pictures. This will facilitate choosing the best photo, the one with all the people smiling, with all of their eyes open, and everyone facing the camera. Carefully store the film containers or memory cards until you can get the film developed or the picture files backed up. Mission pictures are precious and should be taken and preserved with care.

You may also collect mementos, letters, stamps, cartons, can labels, bus receipts, and other items that represent your missionary experience. These should be stored carefully in a sturdy container or box so these items will survive the many transfers you will make and travel home with you to be eventually put in your missionary journal or kept safe in a permanent location.

There will be many other and varied experiences week-to-week, month-to-month, and year-to-year. In all things, remember that what is hard will become easier, what is strange will become familiar, and what is ordinary will become special as you spread the good word of the Gospel.

Go slow, stay focused, and be patient. Keeping a positive attitude will go a long ways towards appreciating the "unusualness" of your ever-changing missionary experience.

Your cheerfulness can make this and all your future life's experiences deeper and more meaningful. It will all work out and some day soon you will be home telling wide-eyed pre-missionaries about all they need to do to prepare for their upcoming mission.

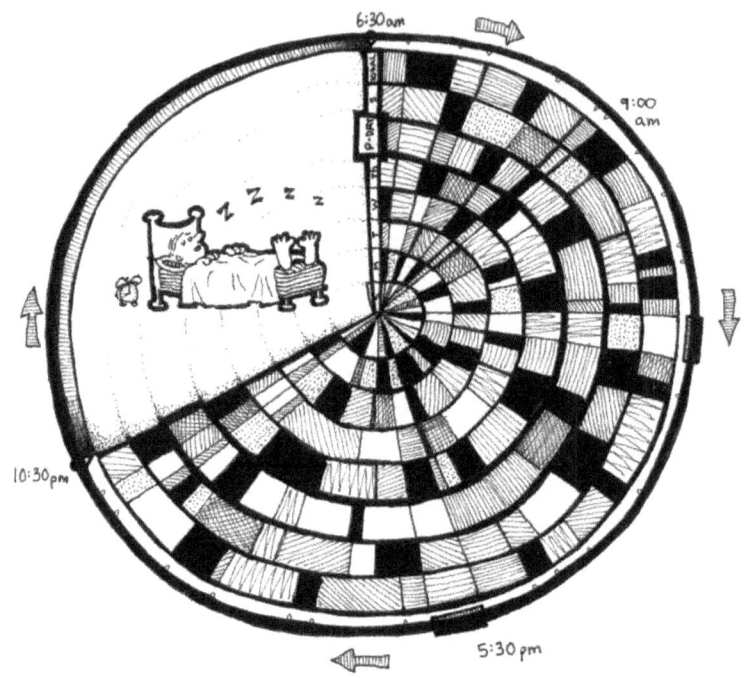

> "[He] did rejoice exceedingly to see his brethren; and what added more to his joy, they were still his brethren in the Lord; yea, and they had waxed strong in the knowledge of the truth; and they were men of a sound understanding and they had searched the scriptures diligently, that they might know the word of God... and when they taught they taught with power and authority of God." Alma 17:2-3

What It Will Be Like

For The Parents –

"I trust parents will remember that their letters to a missionary son or daughter bring home and heaven close to him or to her and provide a renewal of commitment to the sacred calling of missionary. God will inspire you as you take pen in hand to express to one you love the feelings of your soul and the love of your heart." Thomas S. Monson, November 1987 *Ensign*, page 43

Admittedly, sometimes sending a missionary off ends with a sigh of relief. But all too soon, you will need to pay continued attention to your missionary's needs. There are several items to consider.

❑ Letters/Emails.

The single greatest gift your missionary receives while he or she is away is regular, *weekly* communication. This will probably be in the form of a written letter or email while he or she is in the Missionary Training Center and the mission field. Your letters and emails should be motivating, upbeat, and always include your own growing testimony of the Gospel and the blessings you receive because your missionary is serving.

Diligence in writing this regular letter or email is a must. There will be many a week when despite the "things are great" news from your missionary, there will be challenges which he or she chooses not to share. Your regular, weekly message will form a solid foundation of support to look forward to as a lifeline as they learn to cope with a different culture, face challenges with companions, and move from place to place with transfers.

As a side note, most letters to missionaries seem to be written by mothers, which is wonderful. But it cannot be overstated that receiving an occasional letter or email from a missionary dad, preferably once a month or more, can make a tremendous difference in the missionary's capacity to cope, to focus, and to stay in the field. Dads, don't forget your missionary! They need to hear from you directly and frequently, not just obliquely through your wife's letters and emails.

❑ Packages.

Regular packages are also welcome, but be sure to also include your missionary's companion when you mail along gifts. It is better to send to two, then to have a lopsided amount of packages and gifts coming into a companionship.

I sent one of our sons a package of his favorite, homemade cookies. He received the package and happened to open it while taking a long bus ride with other missionaries from his district. He later wrote home that for the first time in his life he felt a strange and wonderful joy from passing out all the cookies to hungry missionaries and only having one himself. This represented a mighty change of heart from selfishness to generosity. It made him a better missionary and a better man!

There are items *not to send*. If your missionary indicates he or she doesn't need this or that, don't keep sending it.

Despite gentle hints to the contrary, I kept sending more unnecessary ties to my last missionary long after he had an abundant supply and would have really preferred some other treat in his occasional package.

There are items *to send*. Candy, especially American candy for a missionary overseas will be relished, shared with children and investigators, and remembered lovingly as the missionary savors the flavors unique to his or her homeland. Also, when you receive specific requests, try to meet them, as sometimes the missionary needs to know you care enough to send along just what they want.

❑ Holidays.

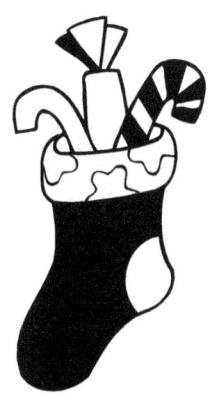

How you choose to celebrate holidays with your missionary will be a very personal decision. However, it is important you and your missionary discuss this before he or she leaves so there are no unmet expectations. And even then, circumstances may preclude you successfully sending regular packages to your beloved missionary.

In our family, we mutually agreed not to send significant birthday or Christmas gifts to our sons while in

Organize for a Mission

the mission field, but would give them these gifts upon their return. This allowed us to carefully choose four gifts that were purchased, wrapped, and presented to them on the day of their return.

At the same time, we chose to mail small, decorative gifts and cards during the year to celebrate their birthdays and other holidays that gave a boost to our missionary's morale. This worked wonderfully well when we could get packages to our missionaries successfully, something that didn't happen until later in our missionary experience, i.e. our first two missionaries rarely got a package we sent, whereas our last two missionaries got every package that was mailed. It just depends on the location of the mission and the local postal system.

There will also need to be some consideration of the time necessary for mailing packages. It is no fun for the missionary to get a Christmas package in the middle of March because you didn't mail it soon enough.

To facilitate sending packages off in a timely manner, I chose to send a trial package soon after our missionaries arrived in the mission field. This gave me a general idea about how much lead-time I needed to get packages prepared and mailed. Then I made written notes on my calendar for the next two years significantly longer then the needed travel time to send off Valentine's Day cards during an early week in January, a small birthday surprise off well before the upcoming birthday, and the holiday decorations package during the early part of November. When I mailed packages

What It Will Be Like

sufficiently ahead of the holidays, our missionaries usually got them before their intended celebrations.

❑ The "Stay-At-Home" Missionary Journals.

As mentioned before, "Stay-At-Home" Missionary Journals should be one of the first preparations made when the mission call comes. This is because there are treasures, letters, and documents that should be immediately and carefully saved. In addition, parents would do well to print a copy of the weekly emails or letters they write while their missionary is in the Missionary Training Center, print emails they write while he or she is in the mission field, make copies of any additional letters they mail, and also print the missionary's weekly emails as they are received. These and any hard copy letters  received from your missionary or the mission home, can be put in the Missionary Journals to give to the missionary when he or she returns.

It is also useful to create and save computer files of the emails for your missionary's journaling needs. From time to time, these files can be "burned" onto a computer CD and kept in a sheet protector in one of the "Stay-At-Home" Missionary Journals.

Photographs and stamps collected from letters and packages can be mounted, and other collectibles can be kept in an orderly manner as they are received.

(See specifics for "Stay-At-Home" Missionary Journal supplies on page 12.)

❑ Correspondence.

With his or her permission, you will need to open and handle mail that will be received after your missionary's departure. Decide how this will be handled so all parties keep their necessary confidentiality and yet this mail is expedited.

❑ Employment, Post-Mission.

While every returned missionary will have different needs, having a temporary job possibility (or even several) upon their return makes for an easier transition for everyone, especially if there is considerable time until school or full-time work starts up again.

About three months before each of our missionaries returned (and with their permission), we began to scout around for possible work by spreading the word our sons would be looking for temporary employment. We were often successful in having several options available when they returned. This was an initial anchor and although they eventually sought and sometimes found other employment that better suited their needs, they had some place to begin.

❑ Feelings, Emotions, and Special Experiences.

One of the surprises for missionary parents is the breadth of emotions they feel during their son or daughter's absence. If it has been a particularly difficult trial during their missionary's teenage years, there may be a certain sense of relief, followed by guilt for feeling such relief, and then often continued concern for the capacities of your son or daughter to be on their own in the mission field.

There will be days when a deep loneliness for your missionary is followed, at times, by a surprisingly number of days when you don't even think about them (which brings up that guilt again). But there are usually other family members close by who need immediate attention, and eventually you will find you pray regularly for your missionary, write them once a week, send an occasional package, and become comfortable with the new situation.

Christmas and Mother's Day calls are emotional highlights, often followed by a day or two of the "dumps" as regular routines return to your life. But the days will pass quickly, especially if you are not focusing on just waiting, but also on your current "nearby" stewardships. Soon enough your missionary will be home again, never to leave for quite so long nor go quite so far away, or so you can hope.

There will likely also be a special spirit in your home during your son or daughter's absence. This experience is hard to describe to someone who hasn't had a missionary out in the field, but when you sense it as you go through your own experience, you will come to appreciate and feel grateful for this blessing. It usually departs upon your missionary's return, only to return again if you have another missionary serve.

❑ Finances.

It is also likely you will be receiving bank statements while your missionary is gone. Using the "Missionary Affairs" Binder, store their bank statements behind the "Finances" tab (as referred to earlier on page 14), make a list of accounts and their locations, and keep other pertinent financial documentation. This will make it much easier to follow and maintain your missionary's personal banking needs for the next eighteen months to two years.

Also, because some monetary gifts, paychecks, or banking account interest might be received after your missionary's departure, it is likely you will be paying tithing for them during their absence. Make sure you are comfortable with how they want these transactions handled. Then, keep careful records in the "Missionary Affairs" Binder of what was done and when.

It seems advantageous to have one of the parent's names added to all banking accounts belonging to the missionary so he or she can move funds around and deposit or withdraw money as needed. For instance, I paid the university tuition from one son's account before his return because the deadline fell before he could focus on this need. We sold one of our son's cars, too, after his departure and were able to put these funds into his account.

It also proved essential to arrange for a debit card in our missionary's name that he took with him. When necessary, we could deposit money into his account here and he would have it accessible wherever he was. We tried at all times to stay within the mission president's guidelines, but this flexibility allowed him to cover additional, unexpected clothing and sundry expenses.

It is possible you will receive several monetary gifts from family members and friends upon your missionary's departure. Discuss and decide with your missionary how this money will best be used: Now for immediate preparation expenses? Put aside for possible unknown mission expenses? Put away for post-mission clothing needs? Put into an account for future family missionary needs?

❑ Housing, Post-Mission.

Depending upon the date of his or her release, parents often make preliminary arrangements for college or other housing before their son or daughter's return. While these decisions will probably be more formally made during the latter part of the missionary's experience and talked about via phone at Christmas or Mother's Day, you may want to make a written note in your planner about discussing these plans or writing about these issues at the appropriate time so they are addressed in a timely manner.

One of our sons wanted to act as a college dormitory assistant upon his return, as this would save him housing expenses. This meant applications being filled out here at home and submitted during the last months of his mission.

Another of our sons wanted us to make a reservation at an apartment complex where his older brothers had stayed so he would be assured of a room. This meant a trip by us to the apartment complex several months before his release, signing papers in his name, and paying the first and last month's rent (plus a deposit).

❏ Rules.

Sometimes, following mission rules is as difficult for the parents as it is for the missionaries. It will be tempting to contact your missionary more often by phone than twice a year, to talk longer than the mission president specifies, and to be more generous with the pocketbook than is required or suggested. In all these ways, parents will benefit from the following the mission rules just as much as their son or daughter.

I remember being informed by our son when we called him one Christmas that the mission president had asked all missionaries to limit their calls to a certain amount of time. This was disappointingly shorter than we had hoped and much shorter than I had wanted. It was a difficult, right-at-the-moment decision we had to make.

Would we or would we not make it easier for our son to be obedient because we also were willing to do so? We could hear the underlying pleading in our son's voice to do as asked, which made it easier to respond accordingly.
When we decided to obey, it was a turning point for us as a family: We would do everything, all the time, to obey the mission rules from our end while they were in the mission field attempting to keep the mission rules, too.

❑ Thank You Notes.

As mentioned before on page 7, the monetary funds received, gifts proffered, and other contributions made towards the missionary's departure will need thank you cards. It is likely that as the parents, one of you will be taking care of this responsibility after your missionary's departure, as he or she will be focused on other things at the Missionary Training Center and then in the mission field. Decide soon when you plan to get this done.

❑ Taxes.

As mentioned earlier on page 14, you will probably be preparing and submitting your son or daughter's state and federal tax returns during their absence. It is important to have the necessary information and paperwork to complete tax returns for the year of your missionary's departure and an understanding that you will complete and submit their returns during their absence.

Keep this information and all other necessary tax paperwork in a "Missionary Affairs" Binder behind the "Taxes" tab so it will be handy as you prepare taxes. You can also store copies of the tax forms you submit in the same place.

❑ Vehicle, Post-Mission.

While every missionary will have different needs and requirements, having an available vehicle for school or work upon his or her return may need consideration. If so, this could be discussed via email or during one of the bi-annual phone calls.

One of our sons lived on campus and didn't need transportation as he returned home right before school began, another lived near campus and rode the bus, a third lived and worked from home during the summer  *after his return and rode a bike when school started, but the fourth son needed reliable transportation for school and work some distance from our home upon his return, so these needs demanded our time and attention during the last months of his mission.*

What It Will Be Like Checklist

- [ ] Letters.
- [ ] Packages.
- [ ] Holidays.
- [ ] "Stay-At-Home" Missionary Journals.
- [ ] Correspondence.
- [ ] Employment, Post-Mission.
- [ ] Feelings, Emotions, and Special Experiences.
- [ ] Finances.
- [ ] Housing, Post-Mission.
- [ ] Rules.
- [ ] Thank You Notes.
- [ ] Taxes.
- [ ] Vehicle, Post-Mission.

It Doesn't End When the Mission Does

"You will shed more tears when you leave to go home than you shed when you left home to come [to the mission]." Gordon B. Hinckley, *Teachings of Gordon B. Hinckley*, page 359

Returning from a mission is almost as challenging as going, both for the missionary and his or her family. There will be a transition period while the missionary "comes" home from his or her memories, a now new "native" cultural background, and the many remembrances. There will be a new, more mature set of siblings with which to rekindle friendships and there will be pleased parents who will be surprised at the maturity which has been obtained, the independence shown, and the testimony gained. All these new interactions and "returning home" experiences take time. Consequently, this chapter is direct to parents.

The missionary will need some time and space to organize his or her missionary papers and treasures. He or she may have some need to label photographs or digital photo files, sort through his or her mementos, make a permanent contact list of missionary companions, investigators, and members.

In addition to the emotional transition and the very real practicalities of the missionary homecoming, the returned missionary will probably also need a "coming home" wardrobe. Some clothes may have been saved and stored from before the mission. Other clothing returning with the missionary will need professional dry cleaning. There will also be needs for new shoes and socks, maybe new underwear, and possibly even new shirts, pants, skirts, and/or blouses.

It would be wise to have some funding for these potential expenses put away before the missionary returns. Plan to spend a little less than one-quarter of what was spent on clothing at the beginning of the mission. This is one expense everyone can look forward to, as the missionary will now be HOME!

There will be many decisions to make, people to see, places to go, and lots of surprising emotions and interactions all around. In addition, it would be wise to inform those you love by letter or email about the missionary's return. To facilitate this homecoming announcement, there follows two example letters to use when announcing the pending homecoming of an Elder or a Sister.

The forms on page 217 and 218 can be also downloaded and printed for your personal use by going to *http://houseoforder.com/category/downloads/*.

Date ____

Dear Family and Friends,

As you may know, our son, ____, will soon complete his missionary service. He will be returning from the ____ mission on ____.

He will be speaking at our sacrament meeting at the ____ building located at ____ on ____ at ____.

We would like to invite you and your family to join us for this special occasion and also for a light meal served after our three-hour block meetings at ____ that same day at our home located at ____.

If you are able to come, we certainly would love to see you, but it not, we fully understand. We are inviting members from both our extended families and several close friends.

We hope to see you, if not on ____, then at any other time you could come by for a visit. We would always be glad to see you if the opportunity presents itself.

Love,

Date ____

Dear Family and Friends,

As you may know, our daughter, ____, will soon complete her missionary service. She will be returning from the ____ mission on ____.

She will be speaking at our sacrament meeting at the ____ building located at ____ on ____ at ____.

We would like to invite you and your family to join us for this special occasion and also for a light meal served after our three-hour block meetings at ____ that same day at our home located at ____.

If you are able to come, we certainly would love to see you, but it not, we fully understand. We are inviting members from both our extended families and several close friends.

We hope to see you, if not on ____, then at any other time you could come by for a visit. We would always be glad to see you if the opportunity presents itself.

Love,

Making It Easier the Next Time Around

"How beautiful are the feet of them that preach the gospel of peace, and bring glad tidings of good things!" Romans 10:15

It is inevitable that as you prepare for this missionary's needs, you may also be thinking ahead to any other "potential" missionaries in your family. This makes good sense. As you do, there are many things to consider. They include involving even young children in saving a small percentage of received money in a "missionary money" jar from the time they begin to regularly receive allowances, monetary gifts, and especially once they begin to earn regular money from summer jobs or babysitting.

And of course, there is nothing like the good example of greeting the missionaries whenever you see them at church or on the street, giving them a loaf of fresh bread from your oven, or inviting them for an occasional meal at your family's table.

Studying the scriptures with your children and encouraging them in their individual scripture study also makes a tremendous difference in personal preparation for the rigors of missionary work. Even occasionally writing letters to "the missionaries" keeps this focus a part of your family's regular routines.

So much of organized missionary preparation begins when they are small, eager, and interested. Speak on a regular basis about missionary work, how you love it, how they will become missionaries some day, and how much you are looking forward to your own "senior" mission. Decide now to be a "missionary mom" and a "missionary dad" with each and every day's activities, focus, and prayer.

In addition to these long-term preparations, there are other important ways for parents to begin now for next time.

Making It Easier the Next Time Around

Do It Once, Twice, or Even Three Times Over

"Establish a house, even a house of prayer, a house of fasting, a house of faith, a house of learning, a house of glory, a house of order, a house of God." D&C 109:8

Whatever you can do now in duplicate or triplicate will save time, trouble, and a learning curve later on.

For instance, because I was preparing recipe cards for my first missionary, I took the time to triplicate my work for my other "future" missionaries. I kept these recipe cards stored until each successive mission call. When the next missionary received his call, the "recipe cards" work was done and easily available for packing. It was one less worry item the next time around.

Also, when I made up family, home, and personal photos and had them laminated for our first missionary, I made additional duplicates for the rest of our "future" missionaries and stored them with the extra sets of recipe cards.

When we found consecrated oil containers on our first shopping trip, we purchased enough for each potential missionary in our family and put them away.

While this may not be the way you choose to "wholesale" plan for your family's missions, we found it was better to have made bulk purchases and have the latest missionary want something different than to be looking, looking, looking for that one item which we remember getting "somewhere" but was no longer conveniently available.

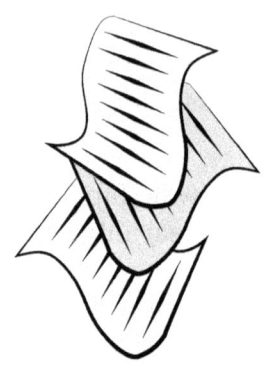

Making It Easier the Next Time Around

Financial Preparations For the Next Missionary

"Set a goal to earn enough money from your part- or full-time work to pay for at ... least a significant part of your mission. I promise great blessings – social, physical, mental, emotional, and spiritual blessings – to every young man [and woman] who pay[s] for a significant part of his [or her] mission." Elder L. Tom Perry, November 2007 Ensign, page 49

It is stressful preparing financially to get a missionary off let alone face the monthly payments that will be a part of your life for the next eighteen months to two years. That being said, if you have other "future" missionaries in your family, it's time to consider setting up interest bearing accounts for each of them and putting away the appropriate amounts into those accounts on a regular basis.

Work with your children so they can consistently add to these missionary accounts as they receive monetary gifts, earn money from part-time jobs, and gain full-time employment. Then, when the next missionary receives his or her call, the financial reserves will be there to send them off.

For instance, if you have a missionary leaving in 24 more months, and you can anticipate his or her mission preparations will cost about $2,000, about $84/month needs to be saved for these needs beginning immediately.

If a second missionary after that will be leaving in approximately four years or 48 months, about $42/month needs to be saved to have about $2,000 for that son or daughter's mission preparation needs.

Begin immediately to save for any younger children who might be going in the future. For example, $12.00/month needs to be saved to have $2,000 in mission preparations needs if your five-year-old son will be going in fourteen years (and this is excluding any interest which may be earned).

It is always easier to save for a longer period of time in small amounts than to come up with big dollars in a short period of time. Start now to make it easier later! Charts with specific amounts to save for different situations can be downloaded for personal use and printing at *http://houseoforder.com/category/downloads/*.

You might even have an experience like my close friend who anticipated his twin sons would serve together, but was surprised when his oldest daughter announced her intentions to go on a mission during the SAME TIME PERIOD. This triple surprise was a little heavy on their family's pocket book. Such financial stresses always seems to occur at the same time as other monetary demands for children's education and marriage. Wisdom seems to dictate starting now to save for then!

In Conclusion ...

"Our missionaries are not salesman with wares to peddle; rather, they are servants of the Most High God, with testimonies to bear, truths to teach, and souls to save." Thomas S. Monson, November 1987 *Ensign*, page 42

Going on a mission is an most interesting and often difficult experiences the missionary and his or her family goes through, especially the first time (well, maybe every time).

Organize for a Mission

There is the excitement of the call, the hard work of getting ready, the fulfillment as final preparations are put in the place, the emotion of departure, the long months of service and separation, and the ecstasy at the missionary's return.

Through it all, you will learn much, make a few mistakes, find answers and form opinions in anticipation for the next missionary's preparations, and finally become a seasoned parent or an experienced returned missionary.

As you become more experienced about missions, please feel free to write me at *marie@houseoforder.com* with your comments, suggestions, and memories. I will incorporate appropriate information into future editions of this book. This will help all of us get more organized for future missions with greater capacity and without so much stress!

Remember, all the forms and checklists in this book can be downloaded and printed for personal use by going to *http://houseoforder.com/category/downloads/*.

May all I have shared make it an easier journey for you and yours! I know our young men and women embark on sacred missions in the name of the Lord, Jesus Christ. I know the Gospel is true and that the Church of Jesus Christ of Latter-day Saints has been restored through the Prophet Joseph Smith. I know each of us has a part in preparing, sending off, supporting and nurturing missionaries.

Because the Gospel is true, may we follow the counsel given, be obedient to the standards set forth, and support missionaries whenever and however we can!

> *"And ye shall go forth in the power of my Spirit, preaching my gospel, two by two, in my name, lifting up your voices as with the sounds of a trump, declaring my word like unto angels of God."* D&C 42:6

About Marie Calder Ricks ...

Marie has been sharing home and professional organization skills for more than 25 years. She began teaching in 1986 at the local community education center where she developed an eight-week, sixteen-topic course including personal organization, time management, food preparation, office and storage organization, budgeting, training children to work, and purchasing skills.

Her classes have proven popular both in San Jose, California and Utah, where she now lives. She frequently teaches organization principles at professional and community gatherings. She also does personal consultations, i.e. she has seen a lot of unkempt offices, cluttered closets, and stacks of untidy paperwork, all of which is very exciting to her.

Marie is a presenter at professional and educational venues all over the United States and has published several books. She has made good use of her personal library that now totals over 300 personal, family, home, and business organization books as she shares valuable and workable ideas in her classes, presentations, and writing.

Marie also writes for various venues, and appears as a featured guest on TV and radio. She has been a radio show host and is the owner of House of Order, a company dedicated to helping men and women find greater organization skills, both in their personal and professional lives. She shares a free, weekly organization newsletter for interested parties. Sign up on her web page, www.houseoforder.com.

Marie also has interests in many other areas. She loves to scrap quilt, make pressed-flower greeting cards for friends and family, and write personal histories.

She is married to Jim Ricks and together they are the parents of five sons. Tom is a Math Education professor at Louisiana State University, David is a emergency medicine resident in Cleveland, Ohio, Brian is a computer science doctoral candidate at Brigham Young University (a husband to Jennifer and father of one), and Tyler is pursuing a degree in animation. (Evan, their youngest, passed away as a young child from leukemia.)

Marie and her husband live in Highland, Utah where they grow a vegetable and fruit garden as their summer hobby and share woodworking projects together on colder days.

Also by Marie Calder Ricks:

ABC Organization, Fun and Easy Life Skills for Children of All Ages
    A fun and colorful children's book teaching 26 simple organization skills.

The Children You Want with the Kids You Have
    200 pages to help parents find better answers to discipline their children, give them a strong work ethic, and have more order at home.

Project Organization: Quick and Easy Ways to Organize Your Life
    170+ pages of effective personal and home organization projects for home managers in all seasons of their lives.

House of Order Handbook
    200+ pages of easy-to-follow instructions for setting up and maintaining an orderly home. This trade paperback includes some 80+ worksheets to help organize your paperwork, finances, and shopping needs. It teaches principles that work!

***House of Order Handbook* CD** 82+ worksheets from the *House of Order Handbook* in .pdf file format for convenient printing on your home computer. It will make keeping organized easier as you complete each and every organization project.

Master Menu Cookbook 50+ spiral bound pages of great, simple recipes to get your Master Menu working every day of the week.

***Stay-At-Home Housecleaning Plan* Packet & Dividers**
    150+ index cards which detail the important daily, weekly, and more complex housework projects to

keep your house neat and clean **plus** 21 laminated, cardstock dividers. *Instructions included.*

***Working Person's Housecleaning Plan* Packet & Dividers** 165+ index cards which detail essential housework projects in a sequential manner to accommodate the more chaotic life while keeping the house clean **plus** 21 laminated, cardstock dividers. *Instructions included.*

***Cleaning Standards* Cards** Five 8-1/2" x 11" heavy-duty laminated sheets, printed on both sides, that detail the essentials needed to get household jobs done right (whether you want the rooms "fast" cleaned, first side, or "deep" cleaned, second side).

***Teaching Children to Work* Packet & Dividers** 150+ index cards which detail the vital skills children and/or teenagers need to survive in the real world as independent adults **plus** 12 laminated, cardstock dividers. *Instructions included.*

***Family Information Binder* Kit** One 1" view binder and 75+ useful printed forms for a family of eight to keep track of the important information needed to run a family. *Instructions included.*

***Organized for the Holidays Binder* Kit** One 1" view binder with instructions, five laminated dividers, 34 forms, and a place for your receipts, ALL to make for a more organized holiday season, this year and every year.

***House of Order* Tutorial CDs** 25 three-minute home organization lessons for using in the CD player in your vehicle or at home (while you wait at soccer games, piano lessons, or any other "down" time).

See **www.houseoforder.com** to order these and other great organizational items.

www.ingramcontent.com/pod-product-compliance
Lightning Source LLC
Chambersburg PA
CBHW071451040426
42444CB00008B/1284